Mutant
Mandarin

时髦汉语

*With best wishes
from James
9/30/95*

王逸之

Other books by James J. Wang

OUTRAGEOUS CHINESE: A Guide to Chinese Street Language
WESTERNERS THROUGH CHINESE EYES

时髦汉语

Mutant Mandarin

A Guide to New Chinese Slang

by

Zhou Yimin & James J. Wang

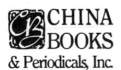

CHINA
BOOKS
& Periodicals, Inc.

To my parents Wang Zhengke and Li Huafeng, who have never said "no" to whatever I've wanted to do.

James J. Wang

Introduction

The Chinese language is mutating. The mutation of language results from the mutating Chinese society. In other words, the fast-changing society has created and is creating situations which are changing people's ways of thinking, and it needs new words to describe events, people, and things. That's why this book is called *Mutant Mandarin*.

Mutant Mandarin attempts to provide a vivid picture of changing China by using the hippest slang terms, complete with detailed interpretations and/or sample sentences. Great efforts have been made to make these examples reflect present-day China's disparate aspects.

Intended to be both a reference book of slang and a source of information about China, it contains the up-to-date slang terms that are being used every day in Beijing as well as in other parts of the country. They are used in all economic and social spheres. Hopefully, with publication of this book, readers will familiarize themselves not only with the mutating language, but with the mutating Chinese society.

This book is based on *Modern Beijing Slang (Beijing Xiandai Liuxingyu)*, a book in Chinese by Mr. Zhou Yimin, Director of Modern Chinese Research Institute at Beijing Normal University. I have redone it in English, and tailored it to Western taste. I want to show thanks, first of all, to Greg Jones, who is always there when I need help, and to Erik Noyes, who provided editorial assistance. Thanks also go to Wendy K. Lee, whose great illustrations and book and cover design have made this book more readable and enjoyable, to Mr. Ma Baolin, my friend and associate, who did a great job of proofreading the manuscript, and to George Felbinger for the title suggestion.

Finally, special thanks go to Dr. Xie Tianwei of the University of California at Davis, Pan Yucheng and Yao Minghui, who assisted with the English-Chinese glossary of new computer terms.

James J. Wang
San Francisco, 1995

Contents

艾滋　*ài zī*　Aids

This term is short for *ài zī bìng* (艾滋病). In Taiwan, it is translated as 爱之病 *ài zhī bìng*, meaning "love disease".

在中国，得艾滋病的人越来越多。
Zài Zhōngguó, dé ài zī bìng de rén yuè lái yuè duō.
In China the number of cases of Aids is on the rise.

安乐死　*ān lè sǐ*　euthanasia, mercy-killing

"安乐死"很难为传统的中国人所接受。
"Ān lè sǐ" hěn nán wèi chuántǒng de Zhōngguórén suǒ jiēshòu.
It is hard for traditional Chinese to accept euthanasia.

拔撞   *báchuàng*   **to back up, to bolster, to increase the prestige of**

The character 撞 is normally pronounced *zhuàng*, but here it is read as *chuàng*.

> 我大哥真给我们拔撞，到那儿就把那几个
> 小子震住了。（他们乖乖地向我们道歉，
> 把拿走的东西原封不动又送回来了。）
> *Wǒ dà gē zhēn gěi wǒmen bá chuàng, dào nàr jiù
> bǎ nà jǐgè xiǎozi zhèn zhù le. (Tāmen guāiguāi de
> xiàng wǒmen dàoqiàn, bǎ ná zǒu de dōngxi yuán
> fēng bú dòng yòu sòng huílai le.*
> My big brother bolstered our image. He sur-
> prised those guys by simply showing up to
> face them. (They apologized to us like well-
> behaved children, and returned to us, intact,
> what they had taken.)

Note: 震住 *zhèn zhù* is also a slang term. It means "to shock", "to surprise", or "to take by storm".

掰 *bāi* to sever (the relationship with), to break up (with)

Literally, this word means "to break something in half".

甭琢磨了，赶紧跟他掰，我就不信你找不着比他强的。

Béng zuómo le, gǎnjǐn gēn tā bāi, wǒ jiù bú xìn nǐ zhǎo bù zháo bǐ tā qiáng de.

Don't think about it any more. Just break up with (dump) him. I'm sure that you'll find someone better.

拜拜 *bái bái* bye-bye, to break up (with)

This term comes from the English word "bye-bye". It has been adopted into the Chinese vocabulary, meaning "to break up with", "to dump" or "to end the relationship with someone".

在他们结婚的前一天，男方突然向女方提出拜拜。

Zài tāmen jiēhūn de qián yìtiān, nánfāng tūrán xiàng nǚfāng tíchū báibái.

The day before his wedding, the man unexpectedly decided to break it off with his fiancee.

我跟她早就拜拜了。

Wǒ gēn tā zǎo jiù báibái le.

I broke up with her a long time ago.

白搭   *báidā*   **no use, no good**

跟她辩也是白搭。
Gēn tā biàn yě shì báidā.
It is no use arguing with her.

白粉   *báifěn*   **drugs, or specifically heroin**

This term literally means "white powder".

他因卖白粉而被枪毙。
Tā yīn mài báifěn ér bèi qiāngbì.
He was executed for selling heroin (or drugs).

摆谱   *bǎipǔ*   **to put on airs, to act conceited; to be haughty**

This term literally means "to showcase (*bǎi*) a certain amount of confidence (*pǔ*)".

想做你就做，不想做你就走人，别跟我这儿摆谱。
Xiǎng zuò nǐ jiù zuò, bù xiǎng zuò nǐ jiù zǒu rén, bié gēn wǒ zhèr bǎipǔ.
If you want to do it, do it; if you don't, you just get out of here. Stop being so conceited. It's obnoxious.

扳大闸   *bān dà zhá*   **to pry open a door (for theft), to burglarize**

这几个坏蛋专门扳大闸，不到三天功夫就偷了二十台电视。

*Zhè jǐgè huài dàn zhuānmén bān dà zhá, bú dào
sāntiān gōngfu jiù tōu le èrshí tái diànshì.*
These thugs specialize in burglary. In the space
of three days, they have stolen twenty TVs.

搬　　*bān*　　**to make (money), to get
(money)**

This word literally means "to move away".

昨天，他被一同道儿搬走人民币八吨半。
*Zuótiān, tā bèi yī tóngdàor bān zǒu rénmínbì bā
dūn bàn.*
Yesterday a guy in the same trade made 8,500
yuan RMB from him.

Note: 吨 *dūn* is also a slang term, meaning one
thousand yuan RMB.

板儿爷 *bǎnr yé*　　**a person that makes
money by riding a tricycle
to deliver goods or pro-
vide taxi service**

办　　*bàn*　　**to punish, to beat up**

你要是再来劲，我们就让人把你办了。
*Nǐ yàoshi zài lái jìn, wǒmen jiù ràng rén bǎ nǐ
bàn le.*
If you keep pressuring us, we'll get someone
to beat you up.

半残废 *bàn cán fèi* a man whose height is not up to standard in women's eyes

This term literally means "half-disabled". Chinese women pay a lot of attention to how tall a man is before deciding to go out with him. Usually a man who is under 5'8" is regarded as "half-disabled" and has a harder time finding a girlfriend than the taller guys.

傍　　*bàng*　　to date; to go out with

她有一个男朋友，但同时又傍着好几个洋人。
Tā yǒu yígè nán péngyou, dàn tóngshí yòu bàngzhe hǎo jǐgè yángren.
She's got a boyfriend, but at the same time she is dating quite a few foreigners on the side.

Note: 洋人 *yángren* means "Westerner" or "foreigner".

傍大款 *bàng dàkuǎn* to depend on (keep company) a man of wealth for money and luxury; to date a rich guy

This term is used on women.

"傍大款"是很多女人追求的人生目标。
"Bàng dàkuǎn" shì hěnduō nǚren zhuīqiú de rénshēng mùbiāo.
"To depend on a wealthy man" is the lifetime goal for a lot of women.

Note: 大款 *dàkuǎn* is also a slang term. It means "a wealthy man or woman".

傍家　*bàngjiā*　lover; mutually dependable partner, friend

1. lover

大款们靠钱财到处物色傍家。
Dàkuǎnmen kào qiáncái dàochù wùsè bàngjiā.
On the strength of their wealth, the rich search low and high for lovers.

2. mutually dependable partner, friend

我跟夏普公司是傍家，不能欺骗别人。
Wǒ gēn xiàpǔ gōngsī shì bàngjiā, bùnéng qīpiàn biéren.
I am a partner of the Sharp Company, so I would never dream of cheating them.

暴侃　*bàokǎn*　to shoot the breeze, to brag wildly, to talk big

到那儿我这一通暴侃，他们都听傻了，真拿我当气功师了。有几位当时就要拜师，让我给他们治病。
Dào nàr wǒ zhè yìtōng bàokǎn, tāmen dōu tīng shǎ le, zhēn ná wǒ dāng qìgōng shī le. Yǒu jǐwèi dāngshí jiù yào bài shī, ràng wǒ gěi tāmen zhìbìng.
After I got there, I completely mesmerized them by talking big, to the point that they began to actually take me for a real qigong master. Some of them even asked me to treat their health problems at any cost.

背黑锅   *bēi hēi guō*   to be a scapegoat

This term literally means "to carry a black wok on one's back".

他做错了事，凭什么让我背黑锅。
Ta zuò cuò le shì, píng shěnme ràng wǒ bēi hēi guō.
You know I did nothing wrong. Why should I be the scapegoat?

北款   *běi kuǎn*   a person of wealth from north China

Literally, this term means "north-wealth".

背   *bèi*   unlucky, especially in gambling

他最近很背，打麻将经常输。
Tā zuìjìn hěn bèi, dǎ májiàng jīngcháng shū.
He has had a string of bad luck lately, losing a lot of money in mahjong games.

毙   *bì*   to reject, to veto

我那本书又让出版社给毙了，告诉说没销路。
Wǒ nà běn shū yòu ràng chūbǎnshè gěi bì le, gàosù shuō méi xiāolù.
My manuscript has been rejected again. The publisher says it just won't sell.

脖儿切 *bór qiē* to give a chop to the neck

The term *bór* means "neck" and *qiē*, "to chop".

他很怕老婆，因为她常常骂他，打他，拧他，
动不动就来个脖儿切。

Tā hěn pà lǎopo, yīnwei tā chángchang mà tā, dǎ tā, níng tā, dòngbúdòng jiù lái gè bór qiē.

He is afraid of his wife, because she often calls him names, beats him, pinches him, and is apt to give him a chop to the neck.

不憷 （怵） *bú chù* fearless, not scared

想去老板那儿告我？赶紧去吧！我可不怵。

Xiǎng qù lǎobǎn nàr gào wǒ? Gǎnjǐn qù ba! Wǒ kě bú chù.

Want to lodge a complaint against me with the boss? Go ahead! I am not scared.

不吝 *bú lìn* not care, not give a damn (about)

只要能去美国，我什么都不吝，搭上一切也
在所不惜。

Zhí yào néng qù měiguó, wǒ shěnme dōu búlìn, dā shàng yíqiè yě zài suǒ bùxī.

As long as I can go to the United States, I don't care if I lose everything.

擦屁股   *cā pìgu*   to wipe one's ass; to finish what is unfinished by someone else

This term means two things. One is the literal act after relieving oneself; the other, to finish something left over by some sloppy person.

都干了几十年编辑了，还要我给你擦屁股。
Dōu gàn le jǐ shí nián biānji le, hái yào wǒ gěi nǐ cā pìgu.
You have been an editor for a few decades. Why are you making me clean up after you now?

残   *cán*   disabled, injured, hurt

Nowadays people like to deliberately exaggerate a little bit when they speak. So when they say "disabled (*cán*)", they don't necessarily mean it.

胡同口那孩子让我给打残了，这下儿再也不敢欺负我们这帮哥们儿了。

Hútong kǒu nà háizi ràng wǒ gěi dǎ cán le, zhè xiàr zài yě bù gǎn qīfu wǒmen zhè bāng gēmenr le.

I beat up the boy living down the alley. Now he is too disabled to bully those buddies of ours.

残废　*cán fèi*

See *bàn cánfèi* 半残废 .

惨　*cǎn*　pitiable, pathetic, in an extremely awkward position

你可别把我跳贴面舞的事登在报纸上，要是让我哥看见，我就惨了。

Nǐ kě bié bǎ wǒ tiào tiēmiàn wǔ de shì dēng zài bàozhǐ shàng, yào shì ràng wǒ gē kànjiàn, wǒ jiù cǎn le.

Don't print in the paper that I was dirty dancing. If my brother read it, I would be in an extremely awkward position.

糙　*cāo*　uncultured, boorish, rough

你这么个年青姑娘怎么能和我们这帮糙人混在一起呢？

Nǐ zhème gè niánqīng gūniang zěnme néng hé wǒmen zhè bāng cāo rén hùn zài yìqǐ ne?

How can a young girl like you blend in with boorish people like us?

操蛋   *cào dàn*   lousy, bad; to bullshit, to talk nonesense

1. lousy, bad

Cào is the equivalent of the English slang word "fuck" or "fucking", and *dàn* means "balls", or "eggs". This expletive can always be used independently, before either a thing or a person, or as a predicate.

你真他妈操蛋，竟当着那么多人的面污辱自己的老婆。

Nǐ zhēn tāmāde càodàn, jìng dāng zhe nàme duō rén de miàn wūrǔ zìjǐ de lǎopo.

You insulted your own wife in front of so many people. You are a fucking bastard!

2. to bullshit, to talk nonsense

你别操蛋了，要是再操蛋，我就废了你丫的。

Nǐ bié càodàn le, yào shì zài càodàn, wǒ jiù fèi le nǐ yā de.

Cut the crap. If you go on bullshitting, I'll beat the shit out of you, son of a bitch.

Note: *Fèi* is a slang term, meaning "to beat the shit out of (somebody)". *Yā de*, short for *yā ting de* (丫挺的), is a slang expletive commonly used by young people, meaning "born to a slave-girl".

操鸡巴蛋   *cào jība dàn*   to bullshit

Jība is the equivalent of the English word "cock" or "dick". For the meaning of *cào* and *dàn*, please see the previous entry. For its usage, please see "*càodàn* (2)".

操性　*càoxing*　**(fucking) nature, disgusting personality, bad moral conduct**

瞧你这操性，还想当经理。
Qiáo nǐ zhè càoxing, hái xiǎng dāng jīnglǐ.
Just have a look at yourself and your disgusting personality. How could you even hope to be the manager?

苯瓦　*cěi*　**ugly-looking**

You would sound very hip if you say *cěi* instead of *chǒu* (丑) when you want to say someone looks ugly. There seems to be a trend that young people deliberately twist their mouth to pronounce certain words.

我们班的女生长得要有多苯瓦就有多苯瓦。
Wǒmen bān de nǚ shēng zhāng de yào yǒu duō cěi jiù yǒu duō cěi.
The girls in our class look as ugly as ugly gets.

苯瓦　*cèi*　**to smash to pieces, to attack, to beat the shit out of**

This term comes from Cantonese.

拳击比赛中，詹姆斯狠狠地苯瓦了乔治。
Quánjī bǐsài zhōng, Zhān Mǔ Sī hěnhěn de cèi le Qiáo Zhì.
In the boxing match, James beat the shit out of George.

蹭   *cèng*   **to enjoy (get) something at others' expense**

他从不掏自己的腰包请客吃饭，总是蹭公家的。

Tā cóng bù tāo zìjǐ de yāobāo qǐngkè chī fàn, zǒngshì cèng gōngjiā de.

He never pays for dinner out of his own pocket but always uses public money.

碴   *chá*   **to come to blows, to get in a fight**

The same as *qiā* (掐)

你怕他干什么，跟他碴，有哥们儿在，你吃不了亏。

Nǐ pà tā gàn shěnme, gēn tā chá, yǒu gēmenr zài, nǐ chī bù liǎo kuī.

Don't be afraid of him. Go ahead and fight him. I'll make sure it is a fair fight.

碴架   *chá jià*   **to get in a fight**

上中学的时候，他经常跟同学碴架。

Shàng zhōngxué de shíhòu, tā jīngcháng gēn tóngxué chá jià.

When he was at high school, he often got into fights with his classmates.

碴舞 *chá wǔ* to dance

Normally the Chinese term for "dance" is *tiàowǔ* (跳舞). The difference is that *chá wǔ* is often used to indicate modern forms like break dancing.

柴火妞儿 *cháihuo niūr* a girl from the countryside

我宁可打光棍也不愿找个柴火妞儿作媳妇。

Wǒ nìngkě dǎ guānggùn yě bú yuàn zhǎo gè cháihuo niū zuò xífu.

I would rather stay single than have a country girl as my wife.

猖 *chāng* furious, unbridled, wild, formidable, uncontrollable

对于卖淫，公安部门所能做的，也不过是掌握监视而已。只要别玩得太猖，公安人员一般都是睁只眼闭只眼。

Duì yú màiyín, gōngān bùmén suǒ néng zuò de, yě búguò shì zhǎngwò jiānshì éryǐ. Zhǐyào bié wán de tài chāng, gōngān rényuán yìbān dōu shì zhēng zhī yǎn bì zhī yǎn.

As for prostitution, the authorities can do nothing but keep a look-out. As long as it doesn't get out of control, the police will do no more than frown upon it.

抄肥　　*chāo féi*　to unfairly profit from a lucrative business; to seize the fruits of business deals by unfair means; to intercept and run away with the booty; to profiteer

我们这车瓜拉到四道口那儿，来了一帮抄肥的，扔给我们二佰块钱就把瓜截跑了。

Wǒmen zhè chē guā lā dào Sìdàokǒu nàr, lái le yìbāng chāo féi de, rēng gěi wǒmen èrbǎi kuài qián jiù bǎ guā jié pǎo le.

While driving this truck loaded with watermelons to Sidaokou, we were intercepted by a group of profiteers, who ran away with all of them after throwing two hundred yuan at us.

抄上了　*chāo shàngle*　run into good luck, have good luck

找到这么漂亮的女朋友，抄上了是不是？

Zhǎo dào zhème piàoliang de nǚ péngyou, chāo shàng le shì bú shì?

You have found yourself such a pretty girlfriend. You have all the luck.

潮　　*cháo*　　trendy, chic, fashionable

她丈夫是做大生意的，所以她才穿得那么潮。

Tā zhàngfu shì zuò dà shēngyì de, suǒyǐ tā cái chuān de nàme cháo.

Her husband is a big time businessman. That is why she dresses so stylishly.

炒　　*chǎo*　　**to repeatedly buy and resell at a profit; to sift again and again to pick the best; to fire, to dismiss**

1. to repeatedly buy and resell at a profit

Literally meaning "to stir-fry", this word is often used together with foreign currency.

他以炒美元为生。
Tā yǐ chǎo měiyuán wéi shēng.
He makes a living by buying and reselling US dollars.

2. to sift again and again to pick the best

新华书店最近炒出了全年十大优畅书。
Xīnhuá shūdiàn zuìjìn chǎo chū le quán nián shí dà yōu chàng shū.
The Xinhua Bookstore recently picked out the ten bestsellers of the year.

3. to fire, to dismiss

See *chǎo yóuyú.*

炒汇　　*chǎo huì*　　**to repeatedly buy foreign currency and resell it at a profit**

不仅在大城市，就是在农村，炒汇的人也大有人在。
Bùjǐn zài dà chéngshì, jiùshì zài nóngcūn, chǎo huì de rén yě dà yǒu rén zài.
Opportunists who buy and resell foreign currency at a profit can be found not only in the big cities but in the countryside.

炒鱿鱼 *chǎo yóuyú*　to dismiss , to fire

This term comes from Cantonese. *Yóuyú* is "squid" in English, and *chǎo*, "stir-fry". When the squid is stir-fried, it rolls up, which figuratively implies "to fold up one's quilt and go home when one is fired."

我在公司里只是一名普通雇员，随时可能被炒鱿鱼。

Wǒ zài gōngsī lǐ zhǐshì yì míng pǔtōng gùyuán, suíshí kěnéng bèi chǎo yóuyú.

I am just a lowly employee in this company. I could get the sack any time.

车倒儿　*chē dǎor* people that buy cars and resell them at a profit

---

撤　　*chè*　to go, to leave, to withdraw

咱们赶紧撤吧，好像要下雨了。

Zánmen gǎnjǐn chè ba, hǎoxiàng yào xià yǔ le.

Let's get out of here. It looks like rain.

撤傍　*chè bàng* to break off the relation-ship or friendship with someone; to stop having anything to do with

约翰逊染上爱滋病毒，许多大公司都在考虑撤傍。

Yuē Hàn Xùn rǎn shàng àizī bìng dú, xǔduō dà gōngsī dōu zài kǎolǜ chè bàng.

Because Magic Johnson was infected with the AIDS virus, many of the big companies that had endorsed him were considering terminating their contracts with him.

臭　　*chòu*　　**stinking, inferior, no good, disappointing; to suck**

中国足球队真臭，连香港都踢不过。
Zhōngguó zúqiú duì zhēn chòu, lián Xiānggǎng dōu tī bú guò.
The Chinese soccer team sucks. It is not even a match for the Hongkong team.

这文章谁写的？真臭！
Zhè wénzhāng shuí xiě de? Zhēn chòu!
Who wrote this article? It really stinks.

臭大粪　　*chòu dà fèn*　　**stinking shit; good-for-nothing**

Dàfèn is "night soil" or "human waste".

日本乒乓球队一个著名选手猛力扣杀，可是球飞向空中，"臭大粪，"我们齐声骂。
Rìběn pīngpāng qiú duì yígè zhùmíng xuǎnshǒu měng lì kòu shā, kěshì qiú fēi xiàng kōng zhōng, "Chòu dà fèn," wǒmen qíshēng mà.
A well-known player on the Japanese table tennis team smashed the ball very hard, but the ball flew over the table. "You stinking shit!" we cursed in unison.

出菜   *chū cài*   productive; to bear fruit, to turn out products

我今年四十五岁，身体健康，阅历丰富。
我觉得现在是我最出菜的时候。

Wǒ jīnnián sìshíwǔ suì, shēntǐ jiànkāng, yuèlì fēngfù. Wǒ juéde xiànzài shì wǒ zuì chū cài de shíhòu.

At the age of forty-five, I am in good health and have the benefit of years of experience. I've never felt more productive.

出血   *chū xuě*   to spend (take out) too much money; to bleed

This term literally means "to bleed".

只要你肯出血，车子房子我都能帮你买。

Zhíyào nǐ kěn chūxuě, chēzi fángzi wǒ dōu néng bāng nǐ mǎi.

As long as you are willing to spend a large amount of money, I can help you buy a car and a house.

他一直很小气，这次让他出点儿血。

Tā yìzhí hěn xiǎoqì, zhècì ràng tā chū diǎnr xuě.

He has always been very stingy. It's only fair that we should bleed him a little bit this time.

床头儿柜   *chúang tóur guì*   a man dominated by his wife, a hen-pecked husband

This term literally means "bedside cupboard". As the character 柜 is homonymous with 跪, or "kneeling", the term is often used to paint a humorous picture of a man who is so afraid of his wife that he kneels by the bedside instead of lying on the bed.

雏儿   *chúr*   **inexperienced person, green-horn, rookie**

妓女瞥了他一眼，知道遇上了一个寂寞难熬的雏儿。

Jìnǔ piē le tā yì yǎn, zhīdào yùshàng le yígè jìmò nán áo de chúr.

The prostitute only glanced at him, and immediately knew that she had run into a lonely, inexperienced client.

呲嗷   *cī'ào*   **to fuck, or a fuck**

People use *cī'ào* rather than *cào* to avoid the offensive sound of the pronunciation of the latter.

磁   *cí*   **very close, intimate**

Cí literally means "magnetic".

我跟他特磁。

Wǒ gēn tā tè cí.

I am very close to him.

磁器   *cíqi*   **buddy, very good friend**

你怎么跟谁都论磁器？
Nǐ zěnme gēn shuǐ dōu lùn cíqi?
How can you treat everyone like they are your best friends?

醋溜儿小生   *cù liūr xiǎo shēng*
a sentimental, wimpy man who usually has a pretty face, an effeminate man

在台湾的电影中，能经常看到满脸泪痕的醋溜儿小生。
Zài Táiwān de diànyǐng zhōng, néng jīngcháng kàndào mǎn liǎn lèihén de cù liūr xiǎo shēng.
In Taiwan movies, you often see effeminate men.

搓麻   *cuō má*   **to mix mahjong tiles; to play mahjong**

搓麻在中国是一种全国性爱好。
Cuō má zài Zhōngguó shì yìzhǒng quánguó xìng àihào.
Playing mahjong is China's national pastime.

搓火　　*cuō huǒ*　　**to get or make anxious (panicky) and angry, to piss off**

遇到这么一个鸡巴人，谁不搓火？

Yùdào zhème yígè jība rén, shuí bù cuō huǒ?

Who wouldn't get pissed off at such a jerk?

Note: For the meaning of *jība*, see *cào jība dàn*. *Jība rén* means "a jerk".

撮　　*cuō*　　**to eat (mostly in a restaurant)**

今天去哪儿撮？

Jīntiān qù nǎr cuō?

Where shall we go to eat today?

打镲   *dǎ chǎ*   **to joke around, to pull one's leg**

这世道！孙女也敢拿她爷爷打镲。
Zhè shìdào! Sūnnǔ yě gǎn ná tā yéye dǎ chǎ.
What has this world come to when even a granddaughter has the guts to pull her grandpa's leg!

打的   *dǎ dī*   **to take a cab**

下班后，她一般都打的回家。
Xiàbān hòu, tā yìbān dōu dǎ dī huíjiā.
After work she usually goes home by taxi.

打水漂　*dǎ shuǐ piāo*　to have one's efforts go to waste; to put in a lot of effort for nothing; to stultify

我给她帮了这么多的忙，投了这么多的钱，看来全打水漂了。

Wǒ gěi tā bāng le zhème duō de máng, tóu le zhème duō de qián, kàn lái quán dǎ shuǐ piāo le.

I have helped her so much and given her so much money, but it seems all this effort has gone to waste.

打住　*dǎ zhù*　to halt, to stop

打住，打住！您别在这儿瞎胡侃了，该干什么干什么去吧。

Dǎ zhù, dǎ zhù! Nín bié zài zhèr xiā hú kǎn le, gāi gàn shěnme gàn shěnme qù ba.

Enough already. Stop talking nonsense here. Go do whatever you are supposed to be doing.

大哥大　*dà gē dà*　cellular phone; the most prestigious person in a group or gang

大件儿 *dà jiànr* **expensive electrical home appliances**

我和你爸结婚的时候，甭说几大件了，连床头柜也是纸糊的。

Wǒ hé nǐ bà jiéhūn de shíhòu, béng shuō jǐ dà jiàn le, lián chuángtóuguì yě shì zhǐ hú de.

When your father and I got married, even the bedside cupboard in the house was wall-papered, to say nothing of expensive electrical appliances.

大款 *dà kuǎn* **a wealthy person**

This term literally means "big money". Now it indicates someone who makes big money.

许多大款扬言，他们能养活好几个老婆。

Xǔduō dàkuǎn yáng yán, tāmen néng yǎng huó hǎo jǐgè lǎopo.

Many wealthy guys brag that they have got enough money to keep several wives.

大团结 *dà tuánjié* **ten-yuan note (yuan: Chinese dollar)**

Dà tuánjié means "great unity". The unity of workers and peasants is pictured on the ten-yuan note.

他从钱包里抽出几张大团结放在桌子上。

Tā cóng qiánbāo li chōu chū jǐ zhāng dà tuánjié fàng zài zhuōzi shàng.

He pulled out several ten-yuan bills and put them on the table.

大腕儿 *dà wànr* celebrity, big shot, authority

许多大男人，一旦有机会同大腕说话，那声音立马变得好温柔好温柔。

Xǔduō dà nánren, yídàn yǒu jīhuì tóng dàwàn shuōhuà, nà shēngyīn lìmǎ biàn de hǎo wēnróu hǎo wēnróu.

A lot of men immediately change their voice to be overly polite and tender when speaking to those of higher authority.

挡横儿 *dǎng hèngr* to block someone's way, won't let pass

怎么着，挡横儿是不是？要想挨练言语一声。

Zěnme zhe, dǎng hèngr shìbúshì? Yào xiǎng ái liàn yán yǔ yì shēng.

What did you mean by that? Trying to stand in my way? If you want to get beaten up, just say the word.

Note: *Ái liàn* is also a slang term, meaning "to be beaten" or "to be hit".

倒汇　*dǎo huì*　to buy foreign currency and resell it at a profit

See *chǎo huì*.

倒儿爷　*dǎor yé*　a person who profiteers from buying and reselling something, racketeer

自从大陆的改革开放以来，倒爷们开始倒腾粮票，鸡蛋票，后来转向外汇，电子产品，手饰，黄色录象等。

Zìcóng dàlù de gǎigé kāifàng yǐlái, dǎoyémen kāishǐ dǎoteng liángpiào, jīdàn piào, hòulái zhuǎnxiàng wàihuì, diànzǐ chǎnpǐn, shǒushì, huáng sè lùxiàng děng.

After the implementation of the open and reform policy in mainland China, racketeers first tried to buy rice and egg coupons and resell them at a profit, and then switched to foreign currency, electronic products, jewelry, and pornographic videos.

灯泡　*dēng pào*　chaperone

Short for 电灯泡 *diàn dēng pào*, this term literally means "electric bulb". Now it is often used to indicate a person who goes out or stays with a couple, and because of his/her presence, the couple have to refrain from doing what they want to.

跟你们俩一起出去？我才不去呢，我最恨当电灯泡了。

Gēn nǐmen liǎng yìqǐ chūqù? Wǒ cái búqù ne, wǒ zuì hèn dāng diàn dēng pào le.

Go out with you two? No way. I hate being a chaperone.

的   *dī*   cab

This word is short for 的士 *dī shì*, which comes from Cantonese.

在宴会上，小赵喝多了。我们赶紧喊来餐厅经理："哥们儿，给叫辆的去呀！"

Zài yànhuì shàng, Xiǎo Zhào hē duō le. Wǒmen gǎnjǐn hǎnlái cāntīng jīnglǐ: "Gémenr, gěi jiào liàng dī qù ya!"

At the banquet, Xiao Zhao got drunk, so we sent for the manager and told him, "Buddy, please call us a cab at once."

的哥   *dī gē*   cab driver, cabby

底儿潮 *dǐr cháo* (to have) criminal records

在大陆，许多底儿潮的人借着经济改革发了财。

Zài dàlù, xǔduō dǐr cháo de rén jiè zhe jīngjì gǎigé fā le cái.

In mainland China, many people with prior criminal records have ridden the wave of economic reform to affluence.

底儿掉   *dǐr diào*   completely exposed, shown inside out, no stone unturned

她把她丈夫虐待孩子的事抖落个底儿掉。
Tā bǎ tā zhàngfu nuèdài háizi de shì dǒu luò gè dǐr diào.
She left no stone unturned in describing how her husband abused their child.

颠儿   *diānr*   to hit the road, to take off

赶紧颠儿吧，要下雪了。
Gǎnjǐn diānr ba, yào xiàxuě le.
Let's hit the road. It's going to snow.

颠菜   *diān cài*   to hit the road, to take off

See *diānr*.

掉价儿 *diào jiàr*   beneath one's dignity, a loss of face

很多名演员都觉得拍广告片掉价儿。
Hěnduō míng yǎnyuán dōu juéde pāi guānggào piān diào jiàor.
Many famous movie stars look upon acting in commercials as being beneath them (disgraceful).

跌份   *diē fèn*   a loss of face, a loss of respect

他认为，在餐馆请客吃饭，如果不多要点儿
菜，就会显得很跌份。

*Tā rènwéi, zài cānguǎn qǐngkè chīfàn, rúguǒ bù
duō yào diǎnr cài, jiù huì xiǎn de hěn diē fèn.*

He deems it a loss of face not to order more
than enough dishes when treating guests to
dinner at a restaurant.

丢份儿 *diū fènr* a loss of face

See *diē fènr*.

斗富 *dòu fù* to contend with someone to see who is more wealthy

The economic reform in China has produced
many upstart entrepreneurs. For historic reasons,
the majority of them are not very well-educated,
but they have the bravado most educated people
lack. As long as there is a potential money-mak-
ing opportunity, they will try it, no matter what
the potential dangers. The last thing these upstarts
want to do is to be looked down upon in any way.
Accordingly, they try to flaunt their wealth whenever an opportunity arises. This results in many
"wars of wealth" in assorted ways between these
upstarts. Some compete in burning money to see
who can afford to burn more, others purchase literally all the fresh flowers in the whole city for
their sweethearts, still others will buy all the seats
in a Karaoke salon just to keep other people out.

逗   *dòu*   **funny, fun, interesting; (expression of skepticism and/or disbelief) come on - get real, you're not serious.**

1. funny, fun, interesting

他这人挺逗的。
Tā zhè rén tǐng doù de.
He is a fun (interesting) person.

2. (expression of skepticism and/or disbelief) come on - get real, you're not serious.

你说她多大？四十岁？别逗了，她只有二十五。
Nǐ shuō tā duō dà? Sì shí suì? Bié dòu le, tā zhí yǒu èr shí wǔ.
How old did you say she is? Forty? Come on, she is only twenty-five.

逗咳嗽   *dòu késou*   **to pick a fight, to go looking for an argument**

This term literally means "to set people coughing".

他不会有什么正经事的，无非找我逗逗咳嗽。
Tā búhuì yǒu shěnme zhèngjing shì de, wú fēi zhǎo wǒ dòu dòu késou.
He didn't come to talk business. He only wanted to pick a quarrel with me.

对路子 *duì lùzi* what someone is doing or has done is precisely his/her forte

他是专门翻译文学的，科技资料不对他的路子。

Tā shì zhuānmen fānyì wénxué de, kējì zīliào bú duì tā de lùzi.

He specializes in literature translation. These scientific and technical materials are not his forte.

吨 *dūn* one thousand yuan (RMB)

今天你要是不掏出八吨，我就剁了你！

Jīntiān nǐ yào shì bù tāo chū bā dūn, wǒ jiù duò le nǐ.

If you don't take out eight thousand yuan today, I'll chop you up.

二把刀   *èr bǎ dāo*   **not skillful enough, not professional enough**

他开车不行，只是个二把刀，每次换道他都需要老婆给他向后看。

Tā kāichē bùxíng, zhǐshì gè èr bǎ dāo, měicì huàn dào tā dōu xūyào lǎopo gěi tā xiàng hòu kàn.

His driving skill needs to be honed. Every time he wants to change lanes, he has to ask his wife to look back for him.

二道贩子 *èr dào fànzi*   **a person that buys and then resells things for a profit**

See *dǎor yé.*

二锅头　*èr guō tóu*　**a person who was once married and is now either widowed or divorced**

This term is also the brand name of the most inexpensive popular hard liquor in Beijing. "*Èr*" means "a second time".

> 是不是因为我是个二锅头，又有两个孩子，所以你不肯嫁给我？
> *Shìbúshì yīnwei wǒ shì gè èr guō tóu, yòu yǒu liǎng gè háizi, suǒyǐ nǐ bù kěn jià gěi wǒ?*
> Is it because I was married once and have two children that you don't want to marry me?

二进宫　*èr jìn gōng*　**to be caught by the police for a second time**

Jìn gōng originally meant "to enter the imperial palace".

> 你知道吗，他这是二进宫了？
> *Nǐ zhīdào ma, tā zhè shì èr jìn gōng le.*
> Do you know that this was the second time he's been arrested?

二倚子　*èr yǐzi*　**having the physical features of both man and woman, hermaphrodite**

发   *fā*   **to make a fortune, to hit the jackpot**

Fā is an abbreviated form of *fācái* 发财.

他一定是发大了，又买车子又买房的。
Tā yídìng shì fā dà le, yòu mǎi chēzi yòu mǎi fáng de.
He must have hit the jackpot. How else could he have bought a car and a house?

反动   *fǎn dòng*   **bad, mean (said in a good-natured way)**

Literally this term means "counter-revolutionary". It is used only in reproach, when you want to say that someone should not have done something.

我们班长真反动，说今晚活动不搞了，白
让我们高兴半天。
Wǒmen bānzhǎng zhēn fǎndòng, shuō jīnwǎn huódòng bù gǎo le, bái ràng wǒmen gāoxìng bàntiān.

Our class monitor is really bad. He said
tonight's activity had been called off. We had
rejoiced for nothing.

方　*fāng*　ten thousand yuan (RMB)

"你到底赢了多少钱？"
"一方外带六棵半。"
"Nǐ dàodǐ yíng le duōshǎo qián?"
"Yì fāng wài dài liù kē bàn."
"How much on earth have you won?"
"Ten thousand six hundred fifty."

Note: 棵 *kē* is also a slang term meaning "one
hundred yuan".

方便　*fāngbiàn*　to urinate or defecate, to use the bathroom

This term literally means "convenience".

对不起，我想方便一下。
Duì bù qǐ, wǒ xiǎng fāngbiàn yíxià.
Excuse me, I'd like to use the bathroom.

房倒儿 *fáng dǎor* a person who helps buy houses for others at a profit (a derogatory term for people who are engaged in the real estate business)

放份儿   *fàng fènr*   **to demonstrate one's power and prestige, to show off**

很明显，这些人就是到这儿放份儿来了。
Hěn míngxiǎn, zhèxiē rén jiùshì dào zhèr fàng fènr lái le.
Without a doubt these people came here to put on a show of their power.

放话儿   *fàng huàr*   **to spread news or rumors, to leak certain information intentionally**

你听见小王往外放话说他是厂长坯子，这厂长非他莫属吗？
Nǐ tīngjiàn Xiǎo Wáng wǎng wài fàng huà shuō tā shì chǎngzhǎng pīzi, zhè chǎngzhǎng fēi tā mò shǔ ma?
Have you heard Xiao Wang spread the rumor that he possesses all the qualities required of a factory director, and that the factory director position belongs to none but him?

放血   *fàng xuě*   **to stab someone, to draw blood**

The term literally means "to let out blood".

小偷晃着手中的刀威胁说："少管闲事，当心老子给你放血。"
Xiǎotōu huàng zhe shǒu zhōng de dāo wēixié shuō: "Shǎo guǎn xiánshì, dāngxīn lǎozi gěi nǐ fàng xuě."

Brandishing the knife in his hand, the thief threatened, "Don't look for trouble, or I'll draw blood from you."

废 *fèi* to beat up, to maim

你要是再敢动我弟弟一根汗毛，我就废了你。
Nǐ yàoshì zài gǎn dòng wǒ dìdi yìgēn hánmáo, wǒ jiù fèi le nǐ.
If you dare to harm a single hair of my brother's head, I'll beat you up.

费 *fèi* to talk nonsense, to bullshit

少跟这儿费！你们家怎么会拿脸盆炖鱼呢？
Shǎo gēn zhèr fèi! Nǐmen jiā zěnme huì ná liǎnpén dùn yú ne?
Cut the crap! How can your family use the face-washing basin to cook fish?

分 *fēn* ten yuan (RMB)

Actually *fēn* is the smallest denomination of *Renminbi*. On gambling tables, however, people have a different psychology toward money, and they have the inclination to treat money like paper. That's why the smallest *fēn* has been elevated to mean a ten-yuan note.

份儿   *fènr*   **good, fine, capable**

爸说杂种狗特份儿！他们跑得快，劲儿足，
而且聪明。

*Bà shuō zázhǒng gǒu tè fènr! Tāmen pǎo de kuài,
jìnr zú, érqiě cōngming.*

Father said that mutts are very capable. They
run fast and are very strong and smart.

佛爷   *fóye*   **pickpocket, thief**

盖 *gài* extremely good, spectacular, better than anything or anybody else

西装一穿，这叫盖！看上去，您简直成了电影名星。

Xīzhuāng yì chuān, zhè jiào gài! Kàn shàng qù, nín jiǎnzhí chéng le diànyǐng míngxīng.

When you put on that suit, you look great! You just look like a movie star.

盖了面积 *gài le miànji* excellent, beautiful, wonderful

我们班王军英语竞赛得了第一，真盖了面积了，可真给咱们学校争光。

Wǒmen bān Wáng Jūn yīngyǔ jìngsài dé le dìyī, zhēn gài le miànji le, kě zhēn gěi zánmen xuéxiào zhēng guāng.

Wang Jun in our class won first place in the English proficiency contest. He was excellent, and his efforts have brought honor to our school.

盖帽儿   *gài màor*   **super, excellent**

球迷们挥动的彩色标语上写着 "中国乒乓球
队盖了帽"。

*Qiúmímen huīdòng de cǎisè biāoyǔ shàng xiě zhe
"Zhōngguó pīngpāng qiú duì gài le mào."*

Sports fans waved colorful flags, which read,
"The Chinese Table Tennis Team Is Super."

敢开牙   *gǎn kāi yá*   **to have the guts to talk big or brag or to say something hard to believe or outrageous**

When crickets bite each other in a fight, it is called
开牙 *kāi yá* (literally meaning "to open one's
teeth").

什么，咱们班你数学最好，你可真敢开牙。
（人家小王参加过国际比赛，还得过奖，都
没敢说这话。）

*Shěnme, zánmen bān nǐ shùxué zuìhǎo, nǐ kě zhēn
gǎn kāi yá. (Rénjia Xiǎo Wáng cānjiā guò guójì
bǐsài, hái dé guò jiǎng, dōu méi gǎn shuō zhè huà.)*

"What, you are the best in math in our class!
How dare you brag so wildly? (Xiao Wang
has participated in the international math
competition and won a prize. Even he doesn't
dare to say so.)

肝儿颤 *gānr chàn* to tremble with fear

Literally the term means "the liver is trembling".

一想到那次车祸他就肝儿颤。
Yì xiǎng dào nàcì chēhuò tā jiù gānr chàn.
He trembled with fear at the thought of his recent car accident.

港纸 *gǎng zhǐ* Hong Kong dollars

高宰 *gāo zǎi* to rip off, to fleece

在中国，外国人经常是小商贩高宰的对象。
Zài Zhōngguó, wàiguóren jīngcháng shì xiǎo shāngfàn gāo zǎi de duì xiàng.
In China, foreigners are often the targets of small retailers who try to rip them off.

搞 *gǎo* to have sex with

他搞过的女人比你看过的女人还多。
Tā gǎoguò de nǚren bǐ nǐ kànguò de nǚren hái duō.
He has slept with more women than you will ever know.

哥们儿 *gēmenr* buddy, home boy

你怎么能出卖你的哥们儿？
Nǐ zěnme néng chū mài nǐ de gēmenr?
How can you betray your home boy like that?

根儿硬 *gēnr yìng* to have strong backing, to have strong people to rely on

小戴的根儿多硬呀，你知道吗，他爸爸是我们市的市长。
Xiǎo Dài de gēnr duō yìng ya, nǐ zhīdào ma, tā bàba shì wǒmen shì de shìzhǎng.
Xiao Dai has formidable backing. You know, his father is mayor of our city.

根儿正 *gēnr zhèng* to have a good moral character

This term was used to mean "to have a good class family background" during the cultural revolution (1966-1976).

他根儿正？你们要是知道他的真实动机，就肯定不会这么想。
Tā gēnr zhèng? Nǐmen yàoshì zhīdào tā de zhēnshí dòngjī, jiù kěndìng búhuì zhème xiǎng.
He has a good moral character? If you knew what his real motive was, you'd think otherwise.

工农兵 *gōng nóng bīng* fifty-yuan RMB note

The term literally means "workers, peasants, and soldiers".

够档次 *gòu dǎng cì*   **up to standard, meeting certain requirements**

国产的小提琴音色好，外观亮，够挡次！
Guó chǎn de xiǎotíqín yīnsè hǎo, wàiguān liàng, gòu dǎngcì.
The domestically made violin is excellent in timbre and beautiful in appearance. It is up to international standards!

官倒儿   *guān dǎor*   **official racketeer**

This new term came into being due to the many instances when government officials took advantage of their public office to engage in buying and reselling at a profit.

官盖   *guān gài*   **unquestionably the best, by far the best, superlative**

鬼市儿 *guǐ shìr*   **market where illegal deals are made at night**

鬼子烟 *guǐzi yān* **cigarettes made in Japan or the United States**

鬼子 *guǐzi*, or devils, has been used by the Chinese to mean foreigners, especially Caucasians and Japanese, for more than a century.

The following is a "Song of a Private Businessman", selected from *Degenerate Men* by Jiang Zilong, a famous Chinese writer. This song vividly illustrates the most fashionable lifestyles individual businessmen are enjoying, and of course, the usuage of *guǐzi* is included therein.

嗅外国蜜，打奔弛的；吸鬼子烟，喝威士忌；穿新潮装，哼流行曲；得爱滋病，洗桑拿浴；炒美元切港币。

Xiù wàiguó mì, dǎ bēn chí dī; Xī guǐzi yān, hē wēi shì jì; Chuān xīn cháo zhuāng, hēng liúxíng qǔ; Dé ài zī bìng, xǐ sāng nà yù; Chǎo měiyuán qiē gǎngbì.

Date foreign darlings, flag down Benz taxis; Smoke foreign cigarettes, drink whisky; Don the latest fashions, hum pop songs; Catch AIDS, take a sauna; Buy and sell US dollars and Hong Kong money.

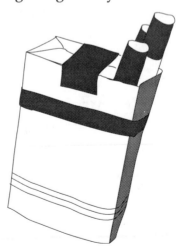

滚大包 *gǔn dà bāo* to steal someone's luggage when he is not looking

他一没技术，二没门道，只能靠"滚大包"生活。
Tā yī méi jìshu, èr méi méndào, zhǐ néng kào "gǔn dà bāo" shēnghuo.
He has neither skills nor social connections, so he has to make a living by stealing luggage.

国际倒儿爷 *guójì dǎor yé* a person who buys in one country and resells in another country for a profit, international racketeer

---

过 *guò* excessive, undue, overly-

做任何事情都不要太过。
Zuò rènhé shìqing dōu bú yào tài guò.
No matter what you do, you shouldn't overdo it.

好　　*hǎo*　　**very, quite, especially**

This usage comes from novels by Qiong Yao, the most famous romance writer in Taiwan. Every one of her novels has been a great success. She is especially popular with teenage girls. When you use *hǎo* instead of *hěn* (很) or *fēicháng* (非常) to modify an adjective, you sound softer and more delicate. It is mostly used by females. More often than not when a male person uses it, he sounds effeminate.

> 她离婚后，日子过得好艰辛好艰辛，活得好寒冷好寒冷。
> *Tā líhūn hòu, rìzi guò de hǎo jiānxīn hǎo jiānxīn, huó de hǎo hánlěng hǎo hánlěng.*
> After she was divorced, she led a very, very hard life, and a very, very cold life.

黑　　*hēi*　　**mean, avaricious, greedy; to cheat, to extort, to blackmail**

1. mean, avaricious, greedy

他们都说长青公司黑，把产品价定得太高。

Tāmen dōu shuō chángqīng gōngsī hēi, bǎ chǎnpǐn jià dìng de tài gāo.

They all say that the Changqing company is greedy because they overprice their products.

2. to cheat, to extort, to blackmail

你黑了人家的钱，今天得拿出一万块来，不然就废了你。

Nǐ hēi le rénjia de qián, jīntiān dé náchū yíwàn kuài lái, bù rán jiù fèi le nǐ.

You have cheated people out of their money. Today you must take out ten thousand yuan. Otherwise we'll beat the shit out of you.

黑道　*hēi dào*　**a gang that engages in illegal activities**

他是黑道上的，最好离他远点儿。

Tā shì hēi dào shàng de, zuì hǎo lí tā yuǎn diǎnr.

He is involved with gangs. We'd better stay away from him.

黑着干 *hēi zhe gàn* **to do unlicensed business ; to do something surreptitiously**

世界各国都有为数不少黑着干的公司。

Shìjiè gèguó dōu yǒu wéi shù bù shǎo hēi zhe gàn de gōngsī.

There are quite a number of unlicensed businesses in every country of the world.

红包   *hóng bāo*   **red envelope containing money, usually used as a gift or for bribery**

每年春节我女儿都能收到许多红包。（有的是爷爷奶奶送的，有的是姑姑叔叔送的，还有的是朋友们送的。）

Měi nián chūnjié wǒ nǚér dōu néng shōudào xǔduō hóngbāo. (Yǒu de shì yéye nǎinai sòng de, yǒu de shì gūgu shūshu sòng de, hái yǒu de shì péngyoumen sòng de.)

Every Spring Festival, my daughter receives a whole bunch of red envelopes. (Some are given to her by her grandparents, some by her aunts and uncles, and others are from our friends.)

呼   *hū*   **to page**

他很少在家，打电话很难找到他，但你可以呼他。

Tā hěnshǎo zài jiā, dǎ diànhuà hěn nán zhǎo dào tā, dàn nǐ kěyǐ hū tā.

It is very hard to reach him by phone since he is seldom at home, but you can page him.

呼机   *hū jī*   **pager, beeper**

花　　*huā*　　horny; to womanize

他人老心不老，花着呢。

Tā rén lǎo xīn bù lǎo, huā zhe ne.

He may be physically old, but not mentally.
He is still as horny as ever.

花了　*huā le*　to beat someone until his head bleeds

你敢害老子，我他妈的花了你！

Nǐ gǎn hài lǎozi, wǒ tāmā de huā le nǐ.

How dare you do harm to me? I'll bash your head in.

会来事　*huì lái shì*　to know how to say appropriate things at the appropriate times

会来事的老婆绝不会当着公婆的面，支使老公干这干那。

Huì lái shì de lǎopo jué búhuì dāng zhe gōngpó de miàn, zhī shǐ lǎogōng gàn zhè gàn nà.

A wife who knows how to do just the right thing never orders her husband around in the presence of his mother.

荤的   *hūn de*   **dirty, obscene**

The word *hūn* literally means "meat or fish", and its antonym is *sù* 素, meaning "vegetable". Used as slang terms, *hūn* means "obscene", and *sù*, "clean".

想听故事？荤的还是素的？
Xiǎng tīng gùshi? Hūn de háishì sù de?
Want to listen to stories? Dirty ones or clean ones?

活儿   *huǒr*   **sexual prowess**

"跟她干过了？"
"干过了。"
"活儿好吗？"
"棒极了。"
"Gēn tā gàn guò le?"
"Gàn guò le."
"Huór hǎo ma?"
"Bàng jí le."
"Have you done the deed with her?"
"Yes."
"How was she?"
"Fantastic."

火   *huǒ*   **prosperous, flourishing; hot, popular**

This word literally means "fire". It can be used in many different contexts. It is very hard to find a satisfactory English equivalent. The word "hot" is similar to *huǒ* in meaning and usage.

你可真火，一年写五本书。

Nǐ kě zhēn huǒ, yì nián xiě wǔ běn shū.

You are obviously very productive, finishing five books in one year.

你可够火的啊，同时傍两个老外。

Nǐ kě gòu huǒ de a, tóngshí bàng liǎng gè lǎo wài.

You're really hot shit, dating two foreigners at the same time.

"他们公司的生意怎么样？"
"特火。"

"Tāmen gōngsī de shēngyì zěnme yàng?"
"Tè huǒ."

"How is their company doing?"
"They are really hot."

加傍   *jiā bàng*   **assistance, cooperation**

芝加哥公牛队本来就很厉害，现在又有麦克·
乔丹加傍，就更加引人注目了。

Zhījiāgē gōng niú duì běnlái jiù hěn lìhài, xiànzài yòu yǒu Màikè Qiáodān jiā bàng, jiù gèn jiā yǐn rén zhùmù le.

The Chicago Bulls are a very tough team. Now with Michael Jordan's help, they will be even more impressive.

假活儿 *jiǎ huór*   **a fake, imitation, cheat**

老王发现那自称为导演的陈某是个假活儿，
整个一个流浪艺人。

Lǎo Wáng fāxiàn nà zìchēng wéi dǎoyǎn de Chén mǒu shì gè jiǎ huór, zhěng gè yígè liúlàng yìrén.

Old Wang found out that Chen was a fake. He claimed to be a movie director, but he was nothing more than a charlatan.

叫板　　*jiào bǎn*　　**to challenge**

"跟我叫板哈？"

"不敢，不敢。您多牛呀，哪敢跟您叫板呀？"

"Gēn wǒ jiào bǎn ha?"

"Bù gǎn, bù gǎn. Nín duō niú ya, nǎ gǎn gēn nín jiào bǎn ya?"

"You want to challenge me, don't you?"

"No, no, we dare not. You are so great! How dare we challenge you?

窖　　　*jiào*　　**to stash away, to hide**

老文把赚来的钱都窖起来了，没人知道放在哪儿。

Lǎo Wén bǎ zhuàn lái de qián dōu jiào qǐlái le, méi rén zhīdào fàng zài nǎr.

Old Wen has hidden all the money he made. No one knows where it is.

姐们儿　*jiě menr*　**buddy (buddies), used among/on female friends**

进局子　*jìn júzi*　**to be arrested by the police**

好些日子不见他来我这儿，问邻居大爷，才知道他进局子了。

Hǎo xiē rìzi bú jiàn tā lái wǒ zhèr, wèn línjū dàye, cái zhīdào tā jìn júzi le.

He never made it to my place. So I checked with an old guy from his neighborhood who told me that he had been arrested by the police.

酒蜜   *jiǔ mì* female drinking companion

巨   *jù*   extremely, exceedingly

这哥们儿巨冒儿，什么都不懂，竟从美国跑
到中国去买瑞士巧克力。

Zhè gēmenr jù màor, shénme dōu bù dǒng, jìng
cóng Měiguó pǎo dào Zhōngguó qù mǎi Ruìshì
qiǎokèlì.*

This guy is extremely stupid. Why else would
he go all the way from the United States to
China to purchase Swiss chocolate?

* See *màor*.

绝活儿 *jué huór*   secret weapon; something one is good at,
unique skill, forte

他的绝活儿到底是什么，我搞不清楚，但我
着实佩服他的毅力。

*Tā de jué huór dàodǐ shì shénme, wǒ gǎo bù
qīngchu, dàn wǒ zhuó shí pèifu tā de yìlì.*

What his secret weapon is, I cannot figure out,
but I do admire him for his willpower.

军蜜   *jūn mì*   a girlfriend who is serv-
ing in the army

开　*kāi*　to dismiss, to fire

This is an abbreviated form of *kāichú* 开除.

他被公司给开了。
Tā bèi gōngsī gěi kāi le.
He was fired by the company.

开刀　*kāi dāo*　to make someone the first target of attack, to make an example of someone, to pick on someone

This term literally means "to go under the knife (to perform or have a surgery)".

有那么多高干受贿，为什么拿我开刀？
Yǒu nàme duō gāo gàn shòuhuì, wèi shénme ná wǒ kāi dāo?
There are so many high-ranking officials taking bribes. Why pick on me?

开涮   *kāi shuàn*   to play around with, to play a trick on

他这人聪明，机灵，热心，谁拿他开涮他都不在乎。

Tā zhè rén cōngming, jīling, rèxīn, shuí ná tā kāi shuàn tā dōu bú zàihu.

He is smart, quick-witted, and warm-hearted. No matter who plays tricks on him, he doesn't get offended.

开洋荤   *kāi yáng hūn*   to enjoy what is enjoyed by foreigners, such as lifestyle, food, and other amenities

肯德鸡、汉堡包、比萨饼长驱直入中国市场，吸引了大批那些以开洋荤为乐的人。

Kěn dé jī, hàn bǎo bāo, bǐ sà bǐng cháng qū zhí rù Zhōngguó shìchǎng, xīyǐn le dàpī yǐ kāi yáng hūn wéi lè de rén.

Speaking of food, Kentucky Fried Chicken, hamburgers and pizzas have pushed their way straight into the Chinese market, alluring those people who take delight in anything foreign.

Note: This term sometimes means "to marry or have sex with a foreign person". For example,

他中国女人玩腻了，想去法国开洋荤。

Tā Zhōngguó nǚren wán nì le, xiǎng qù fǎguó kāi yáng hūn.

He is tired of Chinese women. Now he is interested in going to France to give French women a try.

看瓜　*kàn guā*　(a group of people) to punish (tease) a male person by pulling off his pants to expose his genitals

他上小学的时候，在教室里经常被同学看瓜。

Tā shàng xiǎoxué de shíhòu, zài jiàoshì li jīngcháng bèi tóngxué kàn guā.

When he was attending a primary school, his classmates often teased him by pulling down his pants in the classroom.

侃　*kǎn*　to shoot the breeze, to brag, to boast

他每天什么都不干，就会胡侃。

Tā měitiān shénme dōu bú gàn, jiù huì hú kǎn.

He does nothing but shoot the breeze wildly all day.

侃大山 ***kǎn dà shān***   to shoot the breeze, to brag, to boast

See *kǎn.*

侃价儿 ***kǎn jiàr*** to bargain, to haggle, mostly used when the buyer tries to reduce the price

从南方回北京，不管何时采购，都念念不忘
"侃价"。
Cóng nánfāng huí Běijīng, bùguǎn héshí cǎigòu, dōu niànniàn bú wàng "kǎn jià".
After I came back to Beijing from southern China, I found myself wanting to haggle for a lower price whenever I was shopping.

侃山 ***kǎn shān***   to shoot the breeze, to brag, to boast

See *kǎn dà shān.*

侃爷 ***kǎn yé***   a person who likes, or is good at shooting the breeze, bragging, or boasting

---

棵 ***kē***   one hundred yuan (RMB)

"这事传出去，对谁都没好处！你说个价吧！"
"你看着给吧！"
"五棵行不行？"

"*Zhè shì chuán chūqù, duì shuí dōu méiyǒu hǎochù! Nǐ shuō gè jià ba!*"
"*Nǐ kàn zhe gěi ba!*"
"*Wǔ kē xíng bù xíng?*"
"If this is spread around, it won't do either of us any good. Just give me a price!"
"Make the offer."
"How about five hundred yuan?"

磕　　**kē**　　to stand up to, to fight, to confront with toughness

"要不要找兩人帮帮你？"
"先不用。现在我一个人能对付。反正我是跟他们磕到底了。"

"Yào bú yào zhǎo liǎng rén bāngbang nǐ?"
"Xiān bú yòng. Xiànzài wǒ yí gè rén néng duìfu. Fǎn zhèng wǒ shì gēn tāmen kē dàodǐ le."

"Do you want me to get a few guys to back you up?
"Not now. I think I can stand up to the guys by myself."

磕蜜　**kē mì**　　to chase women, to look for a girlfriend

哥，你真加班么？磕蜜去了吧？
Gē, nǐ zhēn jiā bān me? Kē mì qù le ba?
Brother, did you really work overtime? I bet you were really out chasing girls. Right?

剋斯　　*kēi si*　　**to kiss or a kiss**

From the English word "kiss".

你还记得第次被人剋斯的感觉吗？
Nǐ hái jì dé dì yī cì bèi rén kēi si de gǎnjué ma?
Do you still remember how you felt when you
were first kissed?

空姐儿　　*kōng jiěr*　　**stewardess, female
flight attendant**

款　　*kuǎn*　　**a person of wealth; money**

1. a person of wealth

See *dà kuǎn*.

2. money

知识分子要是没款儿托着，甭打算让人尊重
你。
*Zhīshi fènzǐ yàoshì méi kuǎnr tuō zhe, béng
dǎsuàn ràng rén zūnzhòng nǐ.*
People will never look up to intellectuals if
they don't have any money.

款哥　　*kuǎn gē*　　**a man of wealth**

See *dà kuǎn*.

款姐　　*kuǎn jiě*　　**a woman of wealth**

款爷　*kuǎn yé*　**a man of wealth**

See *dà kuǎn*.

困难　*kùnnan*　**to look ugly, to look miserable**

This term literally means "difficult" or "difficulty". When used to describe a person's looks, it means that the person's appearance is not pretty.

那帮姑娘甭提有多困难了，你不会有兴趣的。
Nà bāng gūniang béng tí yǒu duō kùnnan le, nǐ bú huì yǒu xìngqù de.
Those girls are uglier than any I've ever seen. You won't be interested.

拉   *lá*   **to seduce, to play with; to overcharge, to rip off, to make someone pay more**

1. to seduce, to play with

她太小。你可以随便 "拉" 其他大一点的，
只是别动她。

*Tā tài xiǎo. Nǐ kěyǐ suíbiàn "lá" qítā dà yìdiǎn de,
zhǐshì bié dòng tā.*

She is too young. You may play with other
older women. Just be sure not to touch her.

2. to overcharge, to rip off, to make someone pay more

外国人在北京小摊上买东西，随时都有被
"拉" 的可能。

*Wàiguórén zài Běijīng xiǎo tān shàng mǎi dōngxi,
suíshí dōuyǒu bèi "lá" de kěnéng.*

Foreigners who shop at private vender's
stands are likely to be overcharged any time.

唰　　*lǎ*　　a prostitute

这群 "唰" 经常出没于高级饭店。
Zhè qún "lǎ" jīngcháng chūmò yú gāojí fàndiàn.
This group of prostitutes frequent expensive hotels.

来菜　*lái cài*　　what someone needs has come

The term literally means "The dish has come."

哥们儿，咱们又来菜了。你瞧，他们又往
仓库里放了八台电视，咱们就顺这八台了。
Gēmenr, zánmen yòu lái cài le. Nǐ qiáo, tāmen yòu wǎng cāngkù lǐ fàng le bā tái diànshì, zánmen jiù shùn zhè bā tái le.
They refilled our order and put another eight televisions into the warehouse. Let's walk off with these eight.

Note: Shùn is also a slang term, meaning "to steal".

老爸　*lǎo bà*　　father, daddy

This term is often used by young people.

"老爸，有人找。" 我女儿大声叫到。
"Lǎo bà, yǒu rén zhǎo." Wǒ nǚér dà shēng jiào dào.
"Daddy, you've got a visitor," called my daughter in a loud voice.

老冒儿 *lǎo màor*   **country bumpkin, hick; a slow and clumsy person**

在京城里人们有时把乡下来的人叫 "老冒儿"。
Zài jīng chéng lǐ rénmen yǒushí bǎ xiāng xià lái de rén jiào "lǎo màor".
In the capital city of Beijing, people sometimes call those from the countryside hicks.

老美   *lǎo měi*   **nickname for Americans**

老莫儿 *lǎo mòr*   **specifically the Russian restaurant (*Mò sī kē cāntīng* 莫斯科餐厅), situated in the area of the Exhibition Hall, near the Beijing Zoo and very well known in Beijing**

老泡儿 *lǎo pàor*   **a person who perennially stays at home and doesn't go to work**

Pào means "dawdle", and *lǎo*, "always".

老人家   *lǎo rén jiā*   **Chairman Mao Zedong**

"革命不是请客吃饭，不是做文章......"，
那是老人家说的话。

"Gémìng búshì qǐngkè chīfàn, búshì zuò wénzhāng,......" Nà shì lǎo rén jiā shuō de huà.

"Revolution is not a dinner party, or writing an essay,..." This is what Chairman Mao said.

Note: This term is often used as a respectful form of address for old people.

For example,

您老人家身体好吗？
Nín lǎo rén jiā shēntǐ hǎo ma?
How are you, grandpa (grandma)?

老日　　*lǎo rì*　　**Japanese yen**

他带来了九棵美子，六吨港纸，三方老日。
Tā dài lái le jiǔ kē měi zi, liù dūn gǎng zhǐ, sān fāng lǎo rì.
He brought with him nine hundred US dollars, six thousand Hong Kong dollars, and thirty thousand Japanese yen.

老头儿票　*lǎo tóur piào*　one-hundred yuan bill

On a one-hundred yuan note, there are pictures of four revolutionary leaders. All of them are old. *Lǎo tóur* means "old men".

老外　*lǎo wài*　foreigner; layman

1. foreigner

2. layman

> 你真是个老外！在职职工是不能再申请营业执照的。
>
> *Nǐ zhēn shì gè lǎo wài! Zài zhí zhígōng shì bù néng zài shēnqǐng yíngyè zhízhào de.*
>
> You really don't know anything about this. A person who has already had a job cannot apply for a business license.

雷　*léi*　disaster, catastrophe

This character literally means "thunder".

> 出了事我顶着，雷要炸就炸我一人头上。
>
> *Chū le shì wǒ dǐng zhe, léi yào zhà jiù zhà wǒ yì rén tóu shàng.*
>
> If something bad happens, I'll take it upon myself. If there is a thunder (catastrophe), let it explode only over my head.

雷子   *léizi*   cop

累   *lèi*   **an adjective describing a tiring, tedious and boring life(style) full of restraints**

"真累"，"真烦"成了当今青年人的口头禅。任何时候碰到他们不喜欢的人或事，都会奉上一句"真累"或"真烦"。

"Zhēn lèi", "zhēn fán" chéng le dāngjǐn qīngniánren de kǒu tóu chán. Rènhé shíhòu pèng dào tāmen bù xǐhuān de rén huò shì, dōu huì fèng shàng yí jù "zhēn lèi" huò "zhēn fán".

"That's tiring" or "That is frustrating" has become young people's pet phrase. Whenever they come across people or things not to their liking, they say "It is tiring" or "It is frustrating."

立马儿 *lì mǎr*   **at once, right away**

"要多少钱你给多少钱？要一千，你给吗？"
"没问题，我立马掏。"

"Yào duōshao qián gěi duōshao qián? Yào yìqiān, nǐ gěi ma?"
"Méi wèntí, wǒ lì mǎ tāo."

"You mean no matter how much money I ask for, you are going to give it to me? I want one thousand dollars. Are you going to give that to me?"
"Oh, yes, right away."

练   *liàn*   **to have a competition or fight to see who is better, to fight; to beat**

嘿！小子，看来，我们还没有把你给教训够！是不是再让我练你一回。

"Hèi! Xiǎozi, kàn lái, wǒmen hái méiyǒu bǎ nǐ gěi jiàoxùn gòu! Shì bú shì zài ràng wǒ liàn nǐ yì huí."

"Hey, you pip-squeak! It seems the lesson we taught you was not enough. Do I have to beat you up again?

练摊儿   *liàn tānr*   **to set up a stall to do private business, such as selling books, clothes, and repairing watches**

你不是大牛吗？两年不见怎么练上水果摊了呢？

Nǐ búshì dà niú ma? Liǎng nián bú jiàn zěnme liàn shàng shuǐguǒ tān le ne?

Aren't you Da Niu? I haven't seen you just for two years. How did you end up working at a fruit stand?

零碎儿   *líng suìr*   **filthy language, dirty words, swearwords**

听着，你说话最好别带零碎儿！否则，我把你的嘴撕掉！

Tīng zhe, nǐ shuōhuà zuìhǎo bié dài líng suìr! Fǒuzé, wǒ bǎ nǐ de zuǐ sī diào!

I warn you, you'd better not use that filthy language, or I'll rip your mouth off your face!

溜 *liù* dexterous, adept, skillful, fluent

他电脑玩得挺溜。
Tā diànnǎo wán de tǐng liù.
He is very adept at operating computers.

他英文说得挺溜。
Tā yīng wén shuō de tǐng liù.
He speaks English fluently.

路子 *lùzi* way, method, connections, personal contacts

在中国，没有路子，什么都很难办成。
Zài Zhōngguó, méiyǒu lùzi, shěnme dōu hěn nán bàn chéng.
In China it is extremely hard to get anything done if you don't have connections.

路子野 *lùzi yě* to have many ways and connections (to get something done)

大家都来求你是因为你路子野。
Dàjiā dōu lái qiú nǐ shì yīnwei nǐ lùzi yě.
The reason people come to you for help is that you've got many social connections.

绿的   *lǜde*   US dollars

Literally *lǜde* means "something green". Its present sense results from the green color of US dollars.

乱爱   *luàn ài*   to love recklessly, to love without committment

---

抡   *lūn*   to brag, to talk nonsense, to shoot the breeze

See *kǎn* and *kǎn dàshān*.

码长城 *mǎ chángchéng* **to play mahjong**

When the mahjong pieces are double-layer-stacked, they look much like the well-known Great Wall in China. The character 码 means "to pile up", and 长城, the Great Wall.

买单 *mǎi dān* **to settle accounts, to pay the check (at the restaurant)**

This term comes from Cantonese, but now it is being used almost everywhere. When you eat at a restaurant and want to have the check, you can simply say these words – *mǎi dān* (i.e., May I have the check, please?) – to the server, and the server will bring you your check immediately.

满脸阶级斗争 *mǎn liǎn jiējí dòuzhēng*
to look serious and suspicious of everything

Jiējí dòuzhēng, or class struggle, was often heard before 1976 in China when people distrusted each other. So if you hear "someone's face is all covered with class struggle" (*mǎn liǎn jiējí dòuzhēng*), it means that the person looks suspicious of other people and wears an expression of distrust.

满脸旧社会 *mǎn lǐan jiù shèhuì*
to have a sad expression of bitterness

Jiù shèhuì, or old society, means the pre-1949 China, which is reminiscent of poverty and bitterness. To say "someone's face is all old society" (*mǎn liǎn jiù shè huì*) means that the person looks very pitiable and wretched, with a weather-beaten face, or that he/she is all bitterness and sorrow.

满脸双眼皮 *mǎn liǎn shuāng yǎnpí*
a face full of wrinkles

Shuāng yǎnpí is "double-fold eyelid" in English. Picture a face covered with double-fold eyelids, and you will immediately get a picture of a much wrinkled face.

你不笑还挺年青的，但一笑满脸都是双眼皮。

*Nǐ bú xiào hái tǐng niánqīng de, dàn yí xiào mǎn
liǎn dōu shì shuāng yǎn pí.*
You look young when you don't laugh, but
when you laugh, your face is all covered with
double-fold eyelids (wrinkles).

猫儿匿　*māor nì*　gimmicks, tricks

我一向瞧不起玩猫儿匿的人。什么事情都应
该来明的，而不应来暗的。
*Wǒ yí xiàng qiáo bù qǐ wán māor nì de rén.
Shénme shìqing dōu yīnggāi lái míng de, ér bù
yīng lái àn de.*
I always look down upon those who play
gimmicks. We should do everything in the
open so that we are not accused of being un-
derhanded.

毛片　*máo piān*　pornographic video

This term literally means "fuzzy movie". Pornographic videos are named "fuzzy movies" because they are usually duplicates of duplicates
of duplicates. As pornography is prohibited by
the government, dirty tapes are copied under-
ground.

只要闲着没事，他就和那帮哥们儿聚在一起
看毛片。
*Zhíyào xián zhe méi shì, tā jiù hé nà bāng gēmenr
jù zài yìqǐ kàn máo piān.*
Whenever he was free, he would get together
with his buddies to watch X-rated movies.

冒泡   *mào pào*   the (first) transaction of a business

第一次摆摊做生意时，一连十四天不冒泡，
第十五天一下就卖了一千块钱的货。
*Dì yī cì bǎitān zuò shēngyì shí, yì lián shí sì tiān
bú mào pào, dì shí wǔ tiān yí xià jiù mài le yì qiān
kuài qián de huò.*
When I first started as a vendor at the stand,
there was literally no business for fourteen
consecutive days. On the fifteenth day, however, I sold 1,000 yuan worth of goods.

冒儿   *màor*   stupid; a person who is not mature enough, hick, moron

这位愣管那打火机叫手枪，什么都没见过，
冒儿一个。
*Zhè wèi lèng guǎn nà dǎhuǒjī jiào shǒuqiāng,
shénme dōu méi jiàn guò, màor yí gè.*
This guy insists on calling a lighter a pistol.
He is such an idiot.

冒儿爷   *màor yé*   stupid, uncouth person, hick, moron, idiot

这位老先生，上身穿件西服，下身穿条破裤
子，脚下一双凉鞋，整个一冒儿爷。
*Zhè wèi lǎo xiānsheng, shàngshēn chuān jiàn xīfú,
xiàshēn chuān tiáo pò kùzi, jiǎo xià yìshuāng liáng
xié, zhěng gè yí màor yé.*
Wearing a western-style jacket with torn
pants and a pair of sandals, he looks like a
complete hick.

没劲   *méi jìn*   **meaningless, boring, good-for-nothing**

This term literally means "weak", or "without strength". Everything bad may be called *měijìn* in Chinese.

"电影好看吗？"
"没劲。"
"Diànyǐng hǎo kàn ma?"
"Méi jìn."
"How do you like the movie?"
"Boring."

"你在美国过得怎样？"
"没劲。"
"Nǐ zài Měiguó guò de zěnyàng?"
"Méi jìn."
"How is your life in the United States?"
"Boring."

没脾气   *méi píqi* **to have no control over something and let it go its own way**

真没脾气，眼下姑娘就是喜欢大款，你这穷教授已经不值钱了。
Zhēn méi píqì, yǎn xià gūniang jiù shì xǐhuan dà kuǎn, nǐ zhè qióng jiàoshòu yǐjīng bù zhí qián le.
At present, young women like men of wealth. A poor professor like you is already worthless and you can't do anything about it.

没商量   *méi shāngliang* **not to be altered at all**

"这计划是不是没商量？"
"绝对没商量。"
"Zhè jìhuà shì bú shì méi shāngliang?"
"Juéduì méi shāngliang."
"Isn't this plan to be ameliorated?"
"Absolutely not."

没戏   *méi xì*   **hopeless, impossible; no possibility, no hope**

我这人高不成低不就，看来这辈子是没戏了。
Wǒ zhè rén gāo bù chéng dī bú jiù, kàn lái zhè bèizi shì méi xì le.

I am not competent enough for a high-ranking post and don't want to apply for a lower one. Now I can see no future in my life.

没治   *méi zhì*   **incurable, incorrigible, hopeless; excellent, wonderful**

This term has a high frequency of usage in conversational Chinese, with two totally opposite meanings, as you can see from the following sample sentences.

1. incurable, incorrigible, hopeless

我拿你真没治！叫你往东你偏要往西。
Wǒ ná nǐ zhēn méi zhì! Jiào nǐ wǎng dōng nǐ piān yào wǎng xī.

You are hopeless. When I want you to go east, you insist on going west.

2. excellent, wonderful

"我穿这件衣服好看吗？"
"简直是没治了！"
"Wǒ chuān zhè jiàn yīfu hǎo kàn ma?"
"Jiǎnzhi shì méi zhì le."
"Do I look good in this dress?"
"You look wonderful!"

美丽冻人   *měilì dòng rén*
to dress up without regard for the weather in order to look good

This term is homonymous with 美丽动人, meaning "beautiful and touching".

美子   *měizi*   **US dollars**

门儿清   *ménr qīng*   **to know something clearly, to know something inside and out**

他在中国农村生活了一辈子，对农民的生活全门儿清。
Tā zài Zhōngguó nóngcūn shēnghuó le yí bèi zi, duì nóngmín de shēnghuó quán ménr qīng.
He has lived in the Chinese countryside all his life. He knows everything about the peasants' lives.

眯　　**mī**　　**to stash away, to embezzle, to illegally appropriate**

那一佰块钱肯定被那小子给眯了。
Nà yìbǎi kuài qián kěndìng bèi nà xiǎozi gěi mī le.
That one hundred yuan must have been stolen by that guy.

蜜　　*mì*　　**baby, girlfriend, lover, sweetheart**

我就是二毛的蜜，看着不舒服怎么着？
Wǒ jiùshì Èr Máo de mì, kàn zhe bù shūfu zěnme zhe?"
"Yes, I am Er Mao's girlfriend. Are you jealous?"

面　　*miàn*　　**lacking in courage, cowardly, impotent**

见到强的就向后缩，真他妈的面！
Jiàn dào qiáng de jiù xiàng hòu suō, zhēn tā mā de miàn!
He always runs away when he meets someone stronger. What a coward!

面的　　*miàn dī*　　**van taxi**

In Beijing, a lot of seven-seat vans are used as taxis. They are more popular than others because of their low rates. They used to be one color – yellow; now they are different colors. Usually air-conditioners are not installed, so if you don't have too tight a budget, refrain from using them, especially during the summer months.

面瓜　*miàn guā*　a weak or cowardly person, a slow person, a good-for-nothing

不管谁欺负他，他都不敢吱声，整个一面瓜。
Bùguǎn shuí qīfu tā, tā dōu bù gǎn zhī shēng, zhěnggè yí miàn guā.
When someone bullies him, he doesn't even dare to make a noise. He is a complete coward.

灭　*miè*　puncture the arrogance of, defeat, beat

我不知道李清后来是否灭了对方，只知道我走后她的心情每况愈下。
Wǒ bù zhīdào Lǐ Qīng hòulái shì fǒu miè le duì fāng, zhǐ zhīdào wǒ zǒu hòu tā de xīnqíng měi kuàng yù xià.
I don't know if Li Qing was able to subdue her opponent. The only thing I know is that after I left, her mood went from bad to worse.

名模　*míng mó*　a well-known fashion model

明戏　*míng xì*　to understand, to know, to be clear about

她一进门我就明戏她的来意。
Tā yí jìn mén wǒ jiù míng xì tā de lái yì.
The moment she arrived, I knew why she had come.

木　　*mù*　　**slow, moronic**

　　"我数学又没通过。"
　　"你怎么那么木嘛？"
　　"Wǒ shùxué yòu méi tōngguò."
　　"Nǐ zěnme nàme mù ma?"
　　"I failed in my math again."
　　"How come you are so stupid?"

木瓜　　*mù guā*　　**a stupid person, a slow learner**

嫩　　*nèn*　　young and inexperienced

This word literally means "tender".

他太嫩了，才二十几岁，又没在出版界干过，
怎能负责出版部呢？

*Tā tài nèn le, cái èr shí jǐ suì, yòu méi zài chūbǎn
jiè gàn guò, zěnnéng fùzé chūbǎn bù ne?*

He is too inexperienced: he is in his twenties,
and has never been in the publishing business. How can he be put in charge of the Publishing Department?

牛　　*niú*　　to be swollen with arrogance, to put on airs; to brag, to boast, to talk big

1. to be swollen with arrogance, to put on airs

她怎么也弄不明白，白人为什么这么牛。

*Tā zěnme yě nòng bù míngbai, báiren wèi shénme
zhème niú.*

No matter how hard she tries, she cannot figure out why white people are so arrogant.

2. to brag, to boast, to talk big

这哥们儿能牛着呢，说一见到我就知道我住
哪儿，我什么时候娶的媳妇，这气功也太神
了。

*Zhè gēmenr néng niú zhe ne, shuō yí jiàn dào wǒ
jiù zhīdào wǒ zhù nǎr, wǒ shénme shíhòu qǔ de
xífu, zhè qìgōng yě tài shén le.*

This fellow is really a big talker. He said that
the moment he saw me he knew where I live
and when I got married. This kind of qigong
is way too miraculous to believe.

拍 *pāi* to take something (mostly money) out on the spot; to beat, to defeat; to ingratiate oneself with, to kiss ass

1. to take something (mostly money) out on the spot

他独自一人跑到城里干了半年，回来就给老娘拍出二千块，外带一台大彩电。

Tā dúzì yì rén pǎo dào chéngli gàn le bàn nián, huí lái jiù gěi lǎoniáng pāi chū èrqiān kuài, wài dài yì tái dà cǎidiàn.

He went into town all by himself and worked there for half a year. When he came back, he took out two thousand yuan and gave it to his mother together with a big color TV.

2. to beat, to defeat

许多种子选手这次都被一些无名小卒给拍了
下来。

*Xǔduō zhǒngzi xuǎnshǒu zhècì dōu bèi yìxiē wú
míng xiǎozú gěi pāi le xiàlái.*

This time a lot of seeded players were de-
feated by little-known players.

3. to ingratiate oneself with, to kiss ass

This term is short for 拍马屁 *pāi mǎ pì.*

"他怎么提升得这么快？"
"会拍呗。"

"Tā zěnme tí shēng de zhème kuài?"
"Huì pāi bei."

"How come he has been promoted so fast?"
"Well, he is good at kissing ass."

拍板儿 *pāi bǎnr* to make the final decision

你们公司生意上的事情谁拍板？

*Nǐmen gōngsī shēngyì shàng de shìqing shuí pāi
bǎn?*

Who makes the final business decisions in
your company?

拍婆子 *pāi pózi* to seek women for plea-
sure, to chase women

他是个小色迷，拍婆子有两下子，可也惹出
了不少麻烦。

Tā shì gè xiǎo sè mí, pāi pózi yǒu liǎng xià zi, kě yě rě chū le bù shǎo máfan.

He is a woman chaser. He really knows how to get women, but he also knows how to get into a lot of trouble.

派　　*pài*　　**stylish, hip, chic, cool**

哥们儿，真够派的，你要是在北京开这车，非震倒一大片。

Gēmenr, zhēn gòu pài de, nǐ yào shì zài Běijīng kāi zhè chē, fēi zhèn dǎo yí dà piàn.

It is really cool, buddy. If you drove this car in Beijing, you'd really quake'em down (also a Beijing slang term, meaning "you'd be admired by everybody").

盘儿　*pánr*　**face**

盘儿亮　*pánr liàng*　　**pretty face**

"你觉得那个女人长得怎样？"
"盘儿挺亮的。"

"Nǐ juéde nàgè nǚren zhǎng de zěn yàng?"
"Pánr tǐng liàng de."

"How do you think that woman looks?"
"She's got a pretty face."

坏子   *pīzi*   a person of promise with certain natural endowments

这孩子是唱歌的料，整个一歌星的坏子，好好培养，准有前途。

Zhè háizi shì chànggē de liào, zhěng gè yí gēxīng de pīzi, hǎohao péiyǎng, zhǔn yǒu qiántú.

This child is destined to be a singer. He has all the natural endowments required to be a singer. If he trains properly, he will have a bright future.

痞子   *pǐzi*   ruffian, hoodlum, punk, thug

小痞子们欺负他，揍他，除了哭外，他没什么办法。

Xiǎo pǐzimen qīfu tā, zòu tā, chúle kū wài, tā méi shénme bànfa.

The little ruffians bullied him and hit him. He could do nothing but cry.

片儿汤话   *piànr tāng huà*   socially popular language, slang, street language

这老头离开北京有年头了，可你要是跟他聊起北京的事儿，精神头儿大了，北京的片儿汤话全会。

Zhè lǎotóu líkāi Běijīng yǒu nián tóu le, kě nǐ yào shì gēn tā liáo qǐ Běijīng de shìr, jīngshen tóur dà le, Běijīng de piànr tāng huà quán huì.

This old man has been gone from Beijing for many years. But when you talk to him about Beijing, he becomes very animated, and he knows all the Beijing slang.

票贩子 *piào fànzi* a person who buys tick-
ets and resells them at a
profit; scalper

漂亮姐儿 *piàoliang jiěr* pretty women
(girls)

漂亮妞 *piàoliang niūr* pretty women
(girls)

贫 *pín* garrulous, talkative, long-
winded

这人特贫，一拿起电话就不愿放下。
*Zhè rén tè pín, yì ná qǐ diànhuà jiù bú yuàn fàng
xià.*
This guy is very talkative. Once he picks up
the phone, he never hangs up.

平蹚 *píng tāng* to do whatever one
wants wherever one
goes, to do everything
one's own way

在北京做生意她平蹚。
Zài Běijīng zuò shēngyi tā píngtāng.
When it comes to doing business in Beijing,
she can do whatever she wants whenever she
wants.

平推   *píng tuī*   to sell something at the price at which it was originally purchased without making any profit

起腻　*qǐ nì*　to try to be friendly with, to try to chum up with, to curry favor with, to kiss ass

公司有一帮臭小子天天跟她起腻，哭着喊着要娶她。

Gōngsī yǒu yì bāng chòu xiǎozi tiāntiān gēn tā qǐ nì, kūzhe hǎnzhe yào qǔ tā.

A group of stinking guys in the company tried to chum up with her every day, wailing and whining to marry her.

气管炎　*qì guǎn yán*　wife phobia; a henpecked husband

This term literally means "tracheitis", an inflammation of the windpipe. Because it has the pronunciatin similar to *qī guǎn yán* 妻管严, or "wife's tight control" (over her husband), this term is often used to depict the psychology of a man who is too frightened of his wife. Also see *chuáng tóu guì.*

掐   *qiā*   **to fight**

See *chá*.

枪毙   *qiāng bì*   **to reject, to veto**

See *bì*.

切   *qiē*   **to shortchange, to cheat, to rip off**

This word literally means "to cut", or "to chop". When you shortchange someone, you may be considered to be cutting a piece of flesh off that person. This is why this word is being used in the present sense.

> 十个出汇的，至少有八个让人 "切" 了！
> *Shí gè chū huì de, zhìshǎo yǒu bā gè ràng rén "qiē" le.*
> At least eight out of ten people that sold foreign currency privately have been shortchanged.

切汇   *qiē huì*   **to shortchange someone in the illegal foreign currency swap transactions**

Everywhere in China there are people who make their living by shortchanging people in illegal foreign currency swap transactions. When you find that you have been shortchanged, they know you won't dare to report them, because swapping foreign currency privately is illegal.

轻子 *qīng zi* razors used by thieves for stealing

公安局提醒顾客：购物时谨防"轻子"。

Gōngān jú tíxǐng gùkè: Gòu wù shí jǐn fáng "qīng zi".

The police remind customers to watch out for razors used by thieves when they are shopping.

全活儿 *quán huór* to do everything, to be capable of everything; to work on one job in the daytime and another in the night, wasting no time, to moonlight

1. to do everything, to be capable of everything

他吃喝嫖赌抽，坑蒙拐骗偷，全活儿！

Tā chī hē piáo dǔ chōu, kēn mēng guǎi piàn tōu, quán huór!.

He eats, drinks, womanizes, gambles and smokes, and he cheats, dupes, swindles, deceives, and steals. There is nothing he's not capable of.

2. to work on one job in the daytime and another at night, wasting no time, to moonlight

她白天作保姆，晚上作鸡，全活儿！

Tā báitiān zuò bǎomǔ, wǎnshàng zuò jī, quán huór.

She works as a housekeeper during the daytime, and moonlights as a prostitute at night.

Note: *Jī* is a slang term, literally meaning "chick". Here it means "whore". Compare *jī* with *yā* (鸭), which literally means "duck", and can also be used to mean, "a male prostitute".

惹火　　*rě huǒ*　　**to fire someone's sexual desire, to arouse sexually, to be sexy**

你穿的这条超短裙太惹火了，赶紧换条长点儿的。

Nǐ chuān de zhè tiáo chāoduǎnqún tài rě huǒ le, gǎnjǐn huàn tiáo cháng diǎnr de.

The miniskirt you are wearing is too sexy. Please change to a longer one right away.

惹人　　*rě rén*　　**provocative, sexy and attractive**

亚洲小姐利智素来惹人。

Yǎzhōu xiǎojiě Lì Zhì sù lái rě rén.

Li Zhi, Miss Asia, is always attractive.

人力的   *rén lì dī* rickshaw, tricycle taxi

"人力的"令在北京的旅游者乐不可支。
"Rén lì dī" lìng zài Běijīng de lǚyóuzhě lè bù kě zhī.
"Tricycle taxis" are popular with tourists in Beijing.

人市儿   *rén shìr*   spontaneous labor market

Labor markets are usually organized or premeditated by government agencies. This term stands for a place on which urban unemployed people and people from the countryside spontaneously converge for employment.

中国各地都有许多人市儿。
Zhōngguó gèdì dōuyǒu xǔduō rénshìr.
In different parts of China there are a lot of spontaneous labor markets.

人头儿太次郎 *rén tóur tài cì láng*
a person with bad moral conduct who is disliked by everyone

When you read this term in Chinese, it sounds like a Japanese name.

她业务很好，但很难相处，人头儿太次郎一个！
Tā yèwù hěnhǎo, dàn hěn nán xiāngchǔ, rén tóur tài cì láng yí gè.
Professionally, she is very good, but she is very hard to get along with, and nobody likes her.

软　　*ruá*　　wrinkled, uneven; weak, cowardly, incapable

1. wrinkled, uneven

This character is normally pronounced *ruǎn*, meaning "soft". Used as a slang term, it is read as *ruá*.

> 瞧你，把我的衣服都弄软了，怎么穿？
> *Qiáo nǐ, bǎ wǒ de yīfu dōu nòng ruá le, zěnme chuān?*
> Look at you, you have wrinkled my clothes. How am I going to wear them?

2. weak, cowardly, incapable

> 我早就跟他散了，一点儿男子汉的气派也没有，软得利害，我不喜欢这样的人。
> *Wǒ zǎo jiù gēn tā sàn le, yì diǎnr nánzǐ hàn de qìpài yě méiyǒu, ruá de lìhai, wǒ bù xǐhuān zhè yàng de rén.*
> I dumped him a long time ago. He doesn't have the character that a man should have. He is so weak. I don't like this type.

飒   *sà*   **trendy, sexy and chic; unrestrained and natural in character; having style (mostly used to describe women)**

他对小红一见钟情，宣称一辈子没见过这样绝飒的蜜。
Tā duì Xiǎo Hóng yí jiàn zhōngqíng, xuānchēng yí bèizi méi jiànguò zhèyàng jué sà de mì.
He fell in love with Xiao Hong at first sight, claiming that he had never seen such an absolutely sexy lady.

傻　　*shǎ*　　**to be shocked or stunned because something unexpected happened**

孙强傻了。他万万没想到他老婆的前夫还会从刑场上给救回来。

Sūn Qiáng shǎ le. Tā wànwàn méi xiǎng dào tā lǎopo de qián fū hái huì cóng xíngchǎng shàng gěi jiù huílai.

Sun Qiang was stunned. He never thought that his wife's ex-husband would be rescued from the execution ground.

傻冒儿　*shǎ màor*　**stupid person, idiot; stupid, silly**

See *màor.*

傻青儿　*shǎ qīngr*　**young and inexperienced rash fellow**

晒　　*shài*　　**to leave someone out in the cold, to cold-shoulder, to ignore**

你们都去吃好的喝好的，撒下我不管，成心晒我哪！

Nǐmen dōu qù chī hǎo de hē hǎo de, sā xià wǒ bùguǎn, chéngxīn shài wǒ na!

You guys are going to eat good food and drink good beverages, leaving me behind. You're deliberately ignoring me!

晒干儿 *shài gānr* to leave out, to give the cold shoulder

其实，他比赵亮更难受。他很清楚被晒干儿的正是自己！

Qíshí, tā bǐ Zhào Liàng gèn nánshòu. Tā hěn qīngchu bèi shài gānr de zhèng shì zìjǐ!

But in fact, he felt more miserable than Zhao Liang. He clearly felt that none but he was given the cold shoulder.

煽 *shān* to boast (about), to shoot the breeze, to jabber

哥们儿，行了，别煽了，该打饭去了。

Gēmenr, xíngle, bié shān le, gāi dǎfàn qù le.

O.K., folks! Stop jabbering. It is time to go to get your food.

煽情 *shān qíng* to inflame one's emotion (desire), to emotionally arouse; to flirt or flirtation

1. to inflame one's emotion (desire), to emotionally arouse

这是过节唱的歌，不能太煽情，让观众哭成泪人似的，不大好。

Zhè shì guòjié chàng de gē, bù néng tài shān qíng, ràng guānzhòng kū chéng lèi rén sì de, bú dà hǎo.

This song is going to be sung in celebration of the festival. It shouldn't be too emotional. It is not a good thing to flood the audience's eyes with tears.

2. to flirt or flirtation

你们甭为我着急了，我且得跟她煽情呢。

Nǐmen béng wèi wǒ zhāojí le, wǒ qiě de gēn tā shān qíng ne.

Don't trouble yourselves over me. I'll flirt with her to my heart's content.

什么　*shén mè* **showing disaproval of something**

When 什么 is pronounced *shé mè* rather than *shénme*, it means the speaker is not agreeing with what someone has just said. A lot of young people add a long intonation to *mè* and end the intonation with 呀 *yǎ*.

"那本书写得怎么样？"

"什么呀！"

"Nà běn shū xiě de zěnme yàng?"

"Shénmè ya!"

"What do you think of that book?"

"Oh, what a book! (It is very bad!)

神哨　*shén shào* **to talk big, to boast without any reserve**

这人一张嘴就神哨，能信他？

Zhè rén yì zhāng zuǐ jiù shén shào, néng xìn tā?

Immediately after opening his mouth, this guy starts boasting. How can you believe him?

狮子大张口　*shīzi dà zhāng kǒu*
shockingly greedy, extremely demanding

This term literally means "a lion opens its big mouth." It is used to describe a person who asks for an impossibly huge sum of money when he sets a demand on someone.

什么，五十万！你可真是狮子大张口啊。
Shénme, wǔshí wàn! Nǐ kě zhēnshì shīzi dà zhāngkǒu a.
What, half a million yuan! You are really unbelievably demanding.

屎　*shǐ*　stinking, shitty, bad

This word literally means "shit".

她的麻将打得要多屎有多屎。
Tā de májiàng dǎ de yào duō shǐ yǒu duō shǐ.
She is as bad at playing mahjong as bad can be.

事儿　*shìr*　snoopy, nosy, meddlesome, fussy

你怎么那么事儿？象老太太似的。
Nǐ zěnme nàme shìr? Xiàng lǎo tàitai sì de.
How come you are so fussy? You are just like an old lady.

事儿妈 *shìr mā*   a nosy (fussy) person, a snoop

事儿事儿的   *shìr shìr de*   to appear to be worldly, to seem to be versed in the ways of the world, or look very good at dealing with things and people

瞧她！事儿事儿的，象什么都懂。
Qiáo tā! Shìr shìr de, xiàng shénme dōu dǒng.
Look at her. It seems that she knows how to deal with everything.

手榴弹 *shǒu liú dàn*   high-quality bottled wine given as gifts

This term literally means "hand grenade". It has been associated with bottled wine because they are similar in shape and also because they are both weapons, the latter being the weapon in the war of setting up personal contacts and connections.

刷浆糊 *shuā jiànghu* to ejaculate sperm onto

Few Chinese have their own cars. More than half the population in China travels by bus. Sometimes buses are so crowded that people are squeezed "as thin as their photos". This creates opportunities for sexual perverts to give vent to their suppressed sexual urges. This happens more often in winter, when people are heavily clothed. On a crowded bus, perverts masturbate or rub against a woman, and ejaculate onto her clothes. Because the sperm looks like *jiànghu* (cream-like glue), this indecent behavior is termed *shuā jiànghu* (literally meaning "to brush white glue onto somewhere").

他坐车时总想刷人家浆糊。
Tā zuò chē shí zǒng xiǎng shuā rén jiā jiànghu.
When he takes a bus, he always wants to ejaculate his cream onto female passengers.

刷夜 *shuā yè* to spend the night outside, not at home, suggestive of infidelity

从上中学开始，她就跟着一些不三不四的朋友吃饭馆，刷夜，简直象个坏女孩。
Cóng shàng zhōngxué kāishi, tā jiù gēn zhe yì xiē bù sān bú sì de péngyou chī fànguǎn, shuā yè, jiǎn zhí xiàng gè huài nǚhái.
When she was only a high school student, she began to eat out with her friends of dubious character and spend the night out. She was simply a bad girl.

刷课　*shuà kè*　**to play truant, to skip school**

你这样一周一周的刷课，会跟不上的。
Nǐ zhèyàng yìzhōu yìzhōu de shuā kè, huì gēn bú shàng de.
You skip school week after week. If this continues, you will not be able to catch up with your classmates.

水　*shuǐ*　**of inferior quality, lousy; antonym of 火 *huǒ* (booming), i.e., desolate, unsuccessful, failing**

1. of inferior quality, lousy

办杂志可不容易。一期水点儿，读者就会失望，下期就不买你的。
Bàn zázhì kě bù róngyì. Yì qī shuǐ diǎnr, dúzhě jiù huì shīwàng, xià qī jiù bù mǎi nǐ de.
It is not easy to put a magazine together. If one issue is of inferior quality, its readers will be disappointed and they won't come back to buy the next issue.

2. antonym of 火 *huǒ* (booming), i.e., desolate, unsuccessful, failing

这次书展看来要水了。参展人数怎么这么少。
Zhè cì shūzhǎn kànlái yào shuǐ le. Cān zhǎn rénshù zěnme zhème shǎo?
The book exhibition seems to be a failure this time. How come there is such small attendance?

水货　　*shuǐ huò*　　**smuggled goods**

顺　　　*shùn*　　**to walk off with something, to pick up something on the sly, to steal**

Shùn sounds much better than *tōu* 偷, or "steal". *Tōu* has greater implications like you are committing a crime. If you don't want to put someone down or humiliate that person, you should use *shùn*.

Shùn shǒu qiān yáng 顺手牵羊, a Chinese idiom, means " to lead away a goat in passing". *Shùn*, used in the present sense of stealing, comes from this idiom.

> 顺水果摊上的水果几乎成了他的爱好。
> *Shùn shuǐguǒ tān shàng de shuǐguǒ jīhū chéng le tā de àihào.*
> Stealing fruit from the fruit stand has almost become his hobby.

说摞了　*shuō luò le*　**to make a true complete confession, to blab**

> 我叫你别吱声，你怎么全说摞了？
> *Wǒ jiào nǐ bié zhī shēng, nǐ zěnme quán shuō luò le?*
> I told you to keep quiet. Why did you blab about everything?

死碴   *sǐ chá*   **to fight to the end, to display fortitude**

中国队看来只有和南朝鲜死碴，除此之外没别的路。

Zhōngguó duì kànlái zhǐ yǒu hé Nán Cháoxiǎn sǐ chá, chú cǐ zhī wài méi bié de lù.

The Chinese team looks like they will have no other choice but to fight the South Korean team to the end.

死磕   *sǐ kē*   **to confront someone with death-defying spirit, to fight to the end**

See *sǐ chá.*

死性   *sǐxing*   **inflexible, stubborn**

"你为什么那么死性？他要走就让他走。

Nǐ wèi shénme nàme sǐxing? Tā yào zǒu jiù ràng tā zǒu.

Why are you so stubborn? If he wants to go, let him go.

塔儿哄   *tǎr hòng*   to give someone trouble

我们哥儿几个好不容易凑到一块儿喝两盅儿，你又非得拉他去看电影，你这不是跟我们这儿塔儿哄吗？

Wǒmen gēr jǐgè hǎo bù róngyì còu dào yíkuài hē liǎng zhōngr, nǐ yòu fēi de lā tā qù kàn diànyǐng, nǐ zhè búshì gēn wǒmen zhèr tǎr hòng ma?

My buddies and I have had a hard time getting together to take a few sips of wine. Now you insist on dragging him away to see a movie. Why do you insist on creating such trouble?

抬 *tái* to betray

小地头折过好几次，可谁也没抬过。

Xiǎo Dìtóu zhē guò hǎo jǐcì, kě shuí yě méi tái guò.

Little Ditou was arrested a couple of times, but he had never betrayed anybody.

弹 *tán* to be done for, to be finished

我累弹了。告诉你吧，我吃奶都没费过这么大劲。

Wǒ lèi tán le. Gàosù nǐ ba, wǒ chīnǎi dōu méi fèi guò zhème dà de jìn.

I am dead tired. To tell you the truth, I didn't strain so much muscle when I was suckling from my mom.

蹚混水 *tāng hún shuǐ* to muddle along, to fish in troubled waters

就四个人，现在有三个憋着当经理的，小李不来，说明人家自爱，不蹚这浑水。

Jiù sìgè rén, xiànzài yǒu sāngè biē zhe dāng jīnglǐ de, Xiǎo Lǐ bù lái, shuōmíng rénjia zìài, bù tāng zhè hún shuǐ.

There are only four people here. Now three want to be the manager. Xiao Li didn't show up because he wants to keep out of trouble and doesn't want to muddle along with us.

蹚路子 *tāng lùzi*   **to test the waters, only to have a try**

她是来蹚路子的。
Tā shì lái tāng lùzi de.
She came only to test the waters.

套磁   *tào cí*   **to try to establish a relationship with, to try to get in good with, to kiss ass**

"听口音你我好象是老乡。"
"甭跟我套磁，我哪儿人都不是，我会说十几种方言。"
"Tīng kǒuyīn nǐ wǒ hǎoxiàng shì lǎoxiāng."
"Béng gēn wǒ tào cí. Wǒ nǎr rén dōu búshì. Wǒ huì shuō shí jǐ zhǒng fāngyán."
"Your accent tells me that you and I seem to come from the same place."
"Don't try to kiss my ass. I come from nowhere. I can speak more than ten dialects."

套近乎 *tào jìnhu*   **to try to get in good with someone, to kiss ass**

See *tào cí.*

套儿   *tàor*   **to snare, to trap**

我感觉你们是在给我下套儿。你们也许比我聪明，可我见的多了。
Wǒ gǎnjué nǐmen shì zài gěi wǒ xià tàor. Nǐmen yéxǔ bǐ wǒ cōngming, kě wǒ jiàn de duō le.

I sense you are trying to trap me. I may not be as clever as you are, but I have seen a lot.

特　　*tè*　　**quite, very, especially**

你以为她跟你特铁呀，我当着你的面就可以把她勾搭走。
Nǐ yǐwéi tā gēn nǐ tè tiě ya, wǒ dāng zhe nǐ de miàn jiù kěyǐ bǎ tā gōuda zǒu.
Don't even think she is on especially intimate terms with you. I can seduce her away right in front of you.

提气　　*tí qì*　　**morale boosting, inspirational**

瞧瞧他们的歌唱得多提气！
Qiáo qiáo tāmen de gē chàng de duō tí qì!
Just have a look at how spirit-lifting their singing is!

替　　*tì*　　**money**

Sometimes this character is written as "T".

时间一久，才琢磨出其中的奥妙，关键是没给导游和司机点 "T"。
Shíjiān yì jiǔ, cái zuómo chū qízhōng de àomiào, guānjiàn shì méi gěi dǎoyóu hé sījī diǎn tì.
It was after a long period of time that he figured out that the key to his problem was that he didn't tip the tour guide or the driver.

添堵   *tiān dǔ*   **to add discomfort to, to make someone feel unhappy**

你说这么多不吉利的话不给人添堵？
Nǐ shuō zhème duō bù jílì de huà bù gěi rén tiān dǔ?
Won't your unkind words make people uncomfortable?

添乱   *tiān luàn*   **to bring trouble upon, to exacerbate**

他的担子已经够重了，我们不能为他减轻担子起码不要再给他添乱。
Tā de dànzi yǐjīng gòu zhòng le, wǒmen bù néng wèi tā jiǎnqīng dànzi qǐmǎ búyào gěi tā tiān luàn.
The burden on his shoulders is heavy enough. It is all right that we cannot share the burden, but at least we shouldn't exacerbate his situation.

条儿   *tiáor*   **stature, figure**

这女人条儿很顺。
Zhè nǚren tiáor hěn shùn.
This woman has a good figure.

挑工   *tiǎo gōng*   **to quit one's job**

小刘和老板发生争执，挑工不干了。
Xiǎo Liú hé lǎobǎn fāshēng zhēngzhí, tiǎo gōng bú gàn le.

Xiao Liu got into an argument with his boss, and quit his job as a result.

跳槽　　*tiào cáo*　　**to jump to another work place, to change one's job; to marry someone else after divorce**

1. to jump to another work place, to change one's job

她从外贸局跳槽出来，就没想过再回去。
Tā cóng wài mào jú tiào cáo chùlai, jiù méi xiǎng guò zài huíqù.
She "jumped" out of Foreign Trade Bureau, and never even thought of jumping back.

2. to marry someone else after divorce

离婚不到一年他就跳槽了，这次是跟一个二十岁的大姑娘。
Lí hūn bú dào yì nián tā jiù tiào cáo le, zhècì shì gēn yígè èrshí suì de dà gūniang.
Less than a year after he divorced, he got married again to a woman of only twenty.

贴　　*tiē*　　**to sentence to death**

什么，老木头又折了。这次，他怎么也得贴了。
Shénme, Lǎo Mùtou yòu zhē le. Zhècì, tā zěnme yě de tiē le.
What, Old Mutou has been arrested again! Without a doubt, this time he will be put to death.

铁　　*tiě*　ironclad (relationship), close (relationship), tight

张和刘是同班同学，又是好朋友，关系很铁。
Zhāng hé Liú shì tóng bān tóngxué, yòu shì hǎo péngyou, guānxi hěn tiě.
Zhang and Liu are classmates and good friends. They are very close.

铁磁　*tiě cí*　extremely close and trustworthy friend; on very intimate terms (with)

1. extremely close and trustworthy friend

要不是我跟制片主任是铁磁，你到哪儿找这种好事去？
Yào búshì wǒ gēn zhì piān zhǔrèn shì tiěcí, nǐ dào nǎr zhǎo zhèzhǒng hǎoshì qù?
If the movie producer and I were not good friends, where could you go to find such good deals?

2. on very intimate terms (with)

我和他的关系铁磁，他什么事都给我讲。
Wǒ hé tā de guānxi tiě cí, tā shénme shì dōu gěi wǒ jiǎng.
He and I are really close. He confides everything in me.

铁哥们儿 *tiě gēmenr*　reliable and very close friend

老板雇用他，是因为他是老板铁哥们儿的儿子。

Lǎobǎn gùyòng tā, shì yīnwei tā shì lǎobǎn tiě gēmenr de érzi.
The boss took him in, only because he was the son of a close friend.

铁姐们儿 *tiě jiěmenr* **very reliable and close female friend**

同道儿 *tóng dàor* **a person of the same trade, accomplice**

干这一行，你靠骗人吃饭。你可以骗任何人，就是别骗同道。
Gàn zhè yì háng, nǐ kào piàn rén chī fàn. Nǐ kěyi piàn rènhe rén, jiù shì bié piàn tóng dào.
You live by cheating. You may cheat anybody. But don't cheat people of the same trade.

头头儿脑脑儿 *tóu tour nǎo nǎor*
people in the leadership position

头儿 *tóur* **head, leader, boss**

土鳖 *tǔ biē* **country bumpkin, hick**

See *màor yé* or *màor.*

土得掉渣儿 *tǔ de diào zhār*
**extremely rustic, countrified
(often used to describe one
who behaves or looks very
much like a hick)**

See *màor.*

土老冒儿 *tǔ lǎo màor*   hick

See *màor yé.*

吐血   *tù xiě*   to throw up blood; to bleed

See *chū xuě.*

外国蜜　*wàiguó mì*　lover from another country, foreign lover (woman)

他专嗅外国蜜。
Tā zhuān xiù wàiguó mì.
He only chases foreign women.

玩闹　*wán nào*　rascal, ruffian, social misfit; punk

现在在大陆做生意的很多是以前的玩闹。
Xiànzài zài dà lù zuò shēngyi de hěnduō shì yǐqián de wán nào.
At present in mainland China a lot of people in private business were once social misfits.

玩主儿 *wán zhǔr*　someone who doesn't really work, but who is well-connected and lives a comfortable life

玩儿蛋去   *wánr dàn qù*
to get one's ass out of here

玩儿去   *wánr qù*   to get out of here

玩深沉   *wán shēnchén*
to pretend to be deep or profound

"不清楚，反正古往今来，里里外外，男男
女女的事都有。"
"哟，你也学会玩深沉了？"
*"Bù qīngchu, fǎnzhèng gǔwǎng jīnlái, lǐ lǐ wài
wài, nánnán nǚnǚ de shì dōu yǒu."*
"Yò, nǐ yě xué huì wán shēnchén le?"
"I don't know. Anyway there are stories
about the past and present, ins and outs, men
and women."
"Oh, have you also learnt to be a deep one?"

玩儿稀的   *wánr xīde*   to play a new trick, to
produce something
new

Xīde means "something rare".

最近，他又玩了个稀的，发明了一种新式水
果刀。
*Zuìjìn, tā yòu wán le gè xīde, fāmíng le yìzhǒng
xīnshì shuǐguǒ dāo.*
Recently he came up with something new. He
invented a new type of fruit peeler.

腕儿　　*wànr*　a big shot, a big name

See *dà wànr*.

危　　*wēi*　in jeopardy, in a precarious situation

我老婆发现我跟她的事了，这下可危了。
Wǒ lǎopo fāxiàn wǒ gēn tā de shì le, zhè xià kě wēi le.
My wife has discovered that I was having an affair. This time I am done for.

味儿　　*wèir*　bad smell

美国的公共厕所和中国的一样，味儿着呢！
Měiguó de gōnggòng cèsuǒ hé Zhōngguó de yí yàng, wèir zhe ne!
Public toilets in the US are just like those in China. They have the same bad smell.

味儿事儿　　*wèir shìr*　not good enough, not up to snuff

就你还真象个明星，别人都味儿事儿。
Jiù nǐ hái zhēn xiàng gè míngxīng, biéren dōu wèir shìr.
You are the only one who looks like a movie star. The others aren't up to snuff.

温   *wēn*   **mild, soft, not aggressive**

他是比较温的那一种，很少说话，很怕出事。
Tā shì bǐjiào wēn de nà yìzhǒng, hěn shǎo shuōhuà, hěn pà chū shì.
He is mild mannered. He seldom speaks and is very afraid of causing trouble.

窝儿里斗 *wōr lǐ dòu*   **internal conflict, in-fighting**

窝儿里反 *wōr lǐ fǎn* **struggle among people working or living in the same place, infighting**

五指山 *wǔ zhǐ shān*   **a slap in the face**

This term literally means "Five-finger Mountain". This mountain does exist and stands on China's Hainan Island. Because it is homonymous with 五指扇 *wǔzhǐ shān* (slap with five fingers), the term is used to mean "to box one's ears".

他脾气很不好，动不动就给孩子来几个"五指山"。
Tā píqì hěn bù hǎo, dòng bú dòng jiù gěi háizi lái jǐgè "wǔ zǐ shān."
He has got a bad temper, and often slaps his child in the face.

瞎 *xiā* to find oneself at a loss (as to what to do)

This word literally means "blind", and is short for *zhuāxiā* 抓瞎.

今天多亏了你，要不我就瞎了。
Jīntiān duō kuī le nǐ, yào bù wǒ jiù xiā le.
I am lucky to have you here today, otherwise I would be at a loss as to what to do.

瞎菜 *xiā cài* to find oneself at a loss, to have no way out

这项目没有你的帮助，我们非瞎菜了不可。
Zhè xiàngmu méiyǒu nǐ de bāngzhù, wǒmen fēi xiā cài le bù kě.
We will find ourselves at a loss without your help in this project.

下海　*xià hǎi*　**to plunge into the sea of (private) business**

This term literally means "to go to sea". As a slang term, it means the trend that people who are tired of working for the State-owned enterprises switch to private business.

他下海是因为在国营单位干腻了。
Tā xià hǎi shì yīnwei zài guóyíng dānwèi gàn nì le.
He's started his own business because he is tired of working for the State-owned enterprise.

瞎迷　*xiā mi*　**to find oneself at a loss; no good, to no avail, a waste of one's effort**

1. find oneself at a loss

See 瞎 *xiā*.

2. no good, to no avail, a waste of one's effort

他是头儿，他拍板的事是不会瞎迷的。
Tā shì tóur, tā pāibǎn de shì shì bú huì xiā mi de.
He's the boss. Whatever he has decided won't end up for nothing.

现　*xiàn*　**to make a fool of oneself, to bring shame on, to lose face**

什么，你连这个字都不认识？你可真够现的。
Shénme, nǐ lián zhège zì dōu bú rènshi? Nǐ kě zhēn gòu xiàn de.
What, don't you even know this word? You should be ashamed of yourself.

小打小闹 *xiǎo dǎ xiǎo nào*
to do something in a small place on a small scale

你是做大生意的人，没法跟你比。目前我们只能小打小闹。

Nǐ shì zuò dà shēngyi de rén, méifá gēn nǐ bǐ, mùqián wǒmen zhǐnéng xiǎo dǎ xiǎo nào.

You are doing big business. There's no way for us to compete with you. At present we can only perform limited tasks on a small scale.

小晃儿 *xiǎo huàngr*   little rascal, teenage rascal, punk

小玩闹 *xiǎo wánr nào*   little rascal, teenage rascal, punk

歇菜 *xiē cài*   to give me a break, (want someone) to stop doing something

"你歇菜吧你！就你这种英文水平还想当翻译？"

"Nǐ xiē cài ba nǐ! Jiù nǐ zhè zhǒng yīngwén shuǐpíng hái xiǎng dāng fānyi?"

"Oh, give me a break! How can you possibly become a translator when your English is so bad?

星哥儿   *xīng gēr*   male movie (singing)
                        star

星姐儿   *xīng jiěr*   female movie (singing)
                        star

星儿   *xīngr*   movie (singing) stars

行头   *xíngtou*   one's dress (outfit), the
                    way one is dressed

他打好领带，穿好西服后，问他太太："你
看我这身行头怎么样？"
*Tā dǎ hǎo lǐngdài, chuān hǎo xīfú hòu, wèn tā
tàitai: "Nǐ kàn wǒ zhè shēn xíngtou zěnme yàng?"*
Having done his tie, he put on his Western-
style suit and asked his wife, "What do you
think of my outfit?"

醒   *xǐng*   to wake up to; to be sober-
                minded

赌麻将的时候你们都得醒着点。
*Dǔ májiàng de shíhòu nǐmen dōu de xǐng zhe
diǎn.*
When you gamble in mahjong, you should
be sober-minded.

修长城   *xiū chángchéng*   to play mahjong

See *mǎ chángchéng.*

修理 *xiūli* to teach someone a lesson, to punish

This term, when not used as slang, means "to repair", or "to mend".

他整个一混蛋，修理修理丫的。
Tā zhěngè yī húndàn, xiūli xiūli yā de.
He is an out-and-out scoundrel. Teach this son of a bitch a lesson.

修理地球 *xiū lǐ dì qiú* to till land, to go in for farming

This term literally means "to repair the earth".

嗅蜜 *xiù mì* to chase women, to seek a girlfriend

Xiù literally means "to sniff", or "to take a sniff at". By extension, it means "to sniff out a woman".

许多大款去歌厅并不是为了听歌，而是为了嗅蜜。
Xǔduō dàkuǎn qù gētīng bìng búshì wèile tīng gē, érshì wèile xiùmì.
A lot of wealthy people go to Karaoke bars not to enjoy the music but "to sniff out women".

穴头   *xùe toú*   **organizer of a group of entertainment people to tour around and perform for money**

洋插队 *yáng chā duì* to go overseas to study or work; to work in a foreign country

The term *chā duì* was often used during the Cultural Revolution to mean that educated youth, answering Chairman Mao's call, went to settle down in the countryside. Usually life in the countryside was very tough. *Yáng* means "overseas", or "foreign". Since the early 1980s many Chinese have gone to work or study or settle down in Western developed countries. "*Yáng chā duì*" implies that life in these developed countries is almost as tough as in China's countryside, and the only difference is that by *yáng chā duì*, you may make more money.

洋妞 *yáng niū* foreign girl (woman), foreign chick

洋倒儿爷　*yáng dǎor yé*　foreigners who engage in buying and reselling in China at a profit

This term came into use in the late 1980s when a lot of Russian and East European men and women swarmed into Beijing with big bags. They went on a shopping spree at Beijing's clothes stands, stuffed their bags with all kinds of "fancy things", and then took them back to Russia or other Eastern European countries to resell.

野模　*yě mó*　unprofessional and informal fashion model

页子　*yèzi*　money (bills)

This term literally means "page" or "leaf".

页子活　*yèzi huó*　to be wealthy, to make a lot of money

盘儿亮，页子活，这是九十年代姑娘的择偶标准。

Pánr liàng, yèzi huó, zhè shì jiǔshí niándài gūniang de zé ǒu biāozhǔn.

A man must be handsome and rich to win over a girl of the 1990s.

一个数 *yí gè shù* one hundred yuan

This term literally means "one figure".

这件衣服是最新款式。你要看着好，给一个
数拿走。

*Zhè jiàn yīfu shì zuì xīn kuǎnshì. Nǐ yào kàn zhe
hǎo, gěi yígè shù ná zǒu.*

What do you think of these clothes? They are
the most up-to-date style. If you like them you
can have them for one hundred yuan.

一号儿 *yī hàor* restroom

This term literally means "No. 1".

他实在憋不住了，可附近又没有一号，一下
失去了控制全撒在裤子上了。

*Tā shízài biē bú zhù le, kě fùjìn yòu méiyǒu yī
hào, yí xià shī qù le kòngzhì quán sā zài kùzi shàng
le.*

He couldn't hold it any longer, but there was
no restroom nearby. He lost control and completely wet his pants.

一根儿筋 *yì gēnr jīn* stubborn, as obsti-nate as a mule

Literally the term means "(to have) only one
vein".

遇上这么个一根筋，谁不搓火？

Yù shàng zhème gè yì gēn jīn, shuí bù cuō huǒ?

Who wouldn't be pissed off at such a stubborn person?

一脸旧社会 *yì liǎn jiù shèhuì*
to have a sad expression of bitterness

See *mǎn liǎn jiù shèhuì.*

勇 *yǒng* **bold, brave, courageous**

This term is short for 勇敢 *yǒnggǎn.*

老兄，你还那么勇！刚才一有人冲上去抱那洋妞，我就琢磨是你。
Lǎo xiōng, nǐ hái nàme yǒng! Gāngcai yì yǒu rén chōng shàng qù bào nà yángniū, wǒ jiù zuómo shì nǐ.
Brother, you are still as brave as before! Just now, immediately I saw someone spring on that foreign chick and try to hold her, I thought it must be you.

油倒儿 *yóu dǎor* **a person who buys gasoline or gas coupons and resells at a profit**

有碍市容 *yǒu ài shì róng* **to look ugly or be poorly dressed; (to be) an eyesore**

This term literally means "to affect the appearance of a city".

你就穿这种衣服去参加联欢会呀，太有碍市容了。

*Nǐ jiù chuān zhè zhǒng yīfu qù cānjiā liánhuānhuì
ya, tài yǒu ài shì róng le.*
Are you going to wear those clothes to the
party? You are going to be an eyesore.

有病   *yǒu bìng*   sick, odd, wacky, abnormal

"你有病是不是？大太阳天还打着雨伞。"
"你才有病呢！这不是遮雨，这是遮阳。"
*"Nǐ yǒu bìng shì bú shì? Dà tàiyáng tiān hái dǎ
zhe yǔsǎn."*
*"Nǐ cái yǒu bìng ne! Zhè búshì zhē yǔ, zhè shì
zhē yáng."*
"What's wrong with you? Are you crazy?
Carrying an umbrella on such a sunny day."
"You are the one who is crazy. This umbrella
is for shutting out the sun, not the rain."

有根儿 *yǒu gēnr*   to have (having) strong backing

See *gēnr yìng*.

有戏   *yǒu xì*   very likely, promising; to show promise

The antonym of *méi xì*.

"你认为中国的足球有戏吗？"
"当然有戏。"
"Nǐ rènwéi Zhōngguó de zúqiú yǒu xì ma?
"Dāngrán yǒu xì."
"Do you think China's soccer has a good future?"
"Yes, they show promise."

有一号 *yǒu yí hào*   to occupy a niche (position); to be relatively well-known

现在虽然已经退休，但在人才济济的外交部他仍有一号。

Xiànzài suīrán yǐjīng tuìxiū, dàn zài réncái jìjì de wàijiāobù tā rēn yǒu yí hào.

Although he is retired now, he is still well-known in the Ministry of Foreign Affairs, which boasts a wealth of talents.

淤   *yū*   superfluous, surplus, extra

譬如说，你有五十元钱，淤了。农民要攒起来，工人也许请哥们撮一顿，知识分子咬咬牙，买套工具书。

Pìrú shuō, nǐ yǒu wǔshí yuán qián, yū le. Nóngmin yào zǎn qǐ lai, gōngren yěxǔ qǐng gēmen cuō yí dùn, zhīshi fènzǐ yǎoyao yá, mǎi tào gōngjù shū.

For example, there is fifty yuan extra. The peasant may want to put it in the bank. The worker may use it to treat his friends to dinner. The intellectual may clench his teeth and spend it on a reference book.

晕菜 *yūn cài* confused and disoriented, giddy

一下接触太多的理论，他稍感晕菜。

Yí xià jiēchù tài duō de lǐlùn, tā shāo gǎn yūn cài.

Because he was exposed to so many theories all at once, he felt a little confused and disoriented.

栽   *zāi*   **to lose face, to suffer a set-back, to meet with failure**

他老婆被别人给勾引了。这次他真的栽了。
Tā ǎopo bèi biéren gěi gōuyǐn le. Zhè cì tā zhēn de zāi le.
His wife has been seduced. He has really lost face this time.

宰   *zǎi*   **to overcharge customers when doing business, to rip off**

See *gāo zǎi*.

造　　*zào*　　**to squander**

他把十元当一元花，一顿饭造上一千多元。
Tā bǎ shí yuán dāng yì yuán huā, yídùn fàn zào shàng yìqiān duō yuán.
He spends ten yuan like it's one yuan. He may squander more than one thousand yuan on a single meal.

扎款　*zhā kuǎn*　**to make money, to devise ways to make money**

扎蜜　*zhā mì*　**to chase women, to seek a girlfriend**

See *xiù mì.*

扎势　*zhā shì*　**to foster an image of importance**

你扎势扎得越老，别人就越买你的帐，就越佩服你。
Nǐ zhā shì zhā de yuè lǎo, biéren jiù yuè mǎi nǐ de zhàng, jiù yuè pèifu nǐ.
The more you foster your image, the more respect people will show to you.

渣儿　*zhār*　**fault, problems, a bad record**

乍刺儿 *zhà cìr*   **to be insubordinate; to be disobedient, to go against one's boss**

你真敢不给面子呀！我看看你长着几个脑袋，
跟我这儿乍刺儿。
*Nǐ zhēn gǎn bù gěi miànzi ya! Wǒ kànkan nǐ
zhǎng zhe jǐ gè nǎodài, gēn wǒ zhèr zhà cìr.*
How dare you show no respect to me! I want
to have a look at how many heads you have
grown to have the guts to fight against me.

炸   *zhà*   **to fly into a rage, to explode with rage; to break up (disperse) in a hubbub, to flee in terror**

1. to fly into a rage, to explode with rage

他一听到他被炒的消息，马上就炸了。
*Tā yì tīng dào tā bèi chǎo de xiāoxi, mǎshàng jiù
zhà le.*
As soon as he heard the news that he had been
fired, he exploded with rage.

2. to break up (disperse) in a hubbub, to flee in terror

一帮贼正在屋里分赃，见警察进来，一下子
就炸了。
*Yì bāng zéi zhèngzài wūli fēn zāng, jiàn jǐngchá
jìnlai, yí xià zi jiù zhà le.*
A gang of thieves were dividing the booty in
the room. Suddenly, the police came in, and
the gang fled in all directions.

炸药包 *zhà yào bāo* **packaged goodies or cartons of cigarettes used as gifts**

This term literally means "explosive package". Compare with *shǒu liú dàn*.

张儿 *zhāngr* **ten-yuan bill; (the numeral) ten, mostly used for age**

1. ten-yuan bill

我一个月才挣五张。
Wǒ yí gè yuè cái zhèng wǔ zhāng.
I make only fifty yuan a month.

2. (the numeral) ten, mostly used for age

"有三张了吧？"
"还差几天，下星期天过生日。"
"Yǒu sān zhāng le ba?"
"Hái chà jǐ tiān, xià xīngqī tiān guò shēngri."
"Are you already thirty?"
"A few days short. My birthday will be next Sunday."

长份儿 *zhǎng fènr* to raise one's status and prestige

几年不见，长份儿了，当局长了。
Jǐ nián bú jiàn, zhǎng fènr le, dāng júzhǎng le.
I haven't seen you for years. Your status has changed. Now you are the bureau chief.

长行市 *zhǎng háng shì* to have one's social status undergo a rise; to have higher demands in one's life

女儿在学校英语竞赛得了第一，回来长了行市，对我说："爸，过一年我的英语就会比你好。"
Nǚ'ér zài xuéxiào yīngyǔ jìngsài dé le dìyī, huílai zhǎng le háng shì, duì wǒ shuō: "Bà, guò yìnián wǒ de yīngyǔ jiù huì bǐ nǐ hǎo."
My daughter won first place in the English competition in her school. When she came home, she felt her status had risen. She said to me, "Dad, in one year my English will be better than yours."

照 *zhào* to glare at someone provocatively; business license

1. To glare at someone provocatively

一个小子走上去，"照"了他两眼，然后当胸给了他一拳。
Yí gè xiǎozi zǒu shàng qù, "zhào" le tā liǎng yǎn, ránhòu dāng xiōng gěi le tā yì quán.
One fellow went up, cast a few provocative

glances his way, and then dealt him a blow right to his chest.

2. business license

Short for *zhí zhào* 执照.

找乐 *zhǎo lè* **to seek pleasure, to seek fun**

折 *zhē* **caught in the crime and arrested by the police**

This term literally means "to turn over".

他先后折过三次。
Tā xiān hòu zhē guò sān cì.
He was arrested by the police a total of three times.

折进去 *zhē jìnqu* **to be arrested by the police**

See *zhē*.

震（镇） *zhèn* **to surpass (or surpassing) somebody or something in quality, style, appearance...; to excel; excellent**

我敢说，你的诗集若能出版，肯定震了！
Wǒ gǎn shuō, nǐ de shījí ruò néng chūbǎn, kěndìng zhèn le!
I am pretty sure that if a collection of your poems can be published, it would surpass all

蒸馏水儿衙门 *zhēng liū shuǐr yámen* government institutions that issue very meager bonuses and make little money

Zhēng liǔ shuǐr means "distilled water", and *yámen*, "government office in feudal China", which now is also used to refer to government institutions.

整个儿 *zhěng gèr* out-and-out, downright, complete

This term is mostly used when you say something derogatory.

> 整个一傻冒儿！
> *Zhěng gè yí shǎ mào!*
> An out-and-out fool!

正根儿 *zhèng gēnr* authentic, pure

> 我小市民？我正根的知识分子。清华大学毕业生。
> *Wǒ xiǎo shìmín? Wǒ zhèng gēn de zhīshí fènzǐ.*
> *Qīnghuá dàxué bìyè shēng.*
> What do you mean I am an urban petty bourgeois? I am an authentic intellectual – graduate of Qinghua University.

滋　　*zī*　　comfortable; to ejaculate (prematurely)

1. comfortable

哥们儿，几年不见，活得够滋的呀！都混上大哥大啦，干什么发的财呀？

Gēmenr, jǐ nián bú jiàn, huó de gòu zī de ya! Dōu hùn shàng dà gē dà la, gàn shénme fā de cái ya?

Hi, buddy. Haven't seen you for a couple of years. You look like you are living a comfortable life. You have even got a cellular phone. What have you done to make such a fortune?

2. ejaculate (prematurely)

This word originally meant "to spurt". "To ejacuate" is its extended meaning.

什么，滋了？这么快？你这个没用的东西！

Shénme, zī le? Zhème kuài? Nǐ zhège méi yòng de dōngxi!

What, already done? So fast? You are such a useless thing!

滋润　　*zīrun*　　comfortable

See *zī* (1).

自儿　　*zìr*　　leisurely and carefree, at liberty to enjoy oneself, comfortable

This term is short for 自在 *zìzai*.

走板儿 ***zǒu bǎnr***   **to be different from what is expected or intended, odd, not right, problematic, off key**

"能找两个姑娘吗？" 外国人问出租司机。
"干什么？" 司机觉得有点走板便问。
"Néng zhǎo liǎngge gūniang ma?" Wàiguóren wèn chūzū sījī.
"Gàn shénme?" Sījī juéde yǒu diǎn zǒu bǎn biàn wèn.
"Can you find me some girls?" the foreigner asked the cab driver.
"For what?" said the driver, feeling his passenger's question was a little odd.

走合   ***zǒuhé***   **working as bridge between buyer and seller to make profits from the price difference, a broker**

走穴   ***zǒu xuè***   **(people in the entertainment business) make extra money by going out in temporary groups to give performances here and there**

做　　*zuò*　**to make love**

Euphemism for "to have sex (with)".

你们一星期做几回？
Nǐmen yì xīngqī zuò jǐhuí?
How many times do you do it each week?

Appendix I
Chinese Loan-words

The following terms have been collected in the summer of 1995. We invite readers to submit new terms for subsequent edition of this book.

A

Aids
爱滋（病）
ài zī (bìng)

aspirin
阿司匹林
ā sī pí lín

B

ballet
芭蕾（舞）
bā léi (wǔ)

bar
酒吧，吧
jiǔ bā, bā

beeper
BP机
bì pì jī

beer
啤酒
pí jiǔ

Benz
奔驰
bēn chí

bikini
比基尼
bǐ jī ní

BMW
宝马
bǎo mǎ

Boeing
波音
bō yīn

bowling	保龄球
	bǎo líng qiú
brandy	白兰地
	bái lán dì
buffet	布斐
	bù fēi
bus	巴士
	bā shì
bye-bye	拜拜
	bái bái

C

carat	克拉
	kè lā
cashmere	开士米
	kāi shì mǐ
champagne	香槟
	xiāng bīn
chocolate	巧克力
	qiǎo kè lì
cigar	雪茄
	xuě jiā
coca cola	可口可乐
	kě kǒu kě lè
cocaine	可卡因
	kě kǎ yīn
coffee	咖啡
	kā fēi
Contac	康泰克
	kāng tài kè

D

| disco | 迪斯科 |
| | *dí sī kē* |

F

fascist	法西斯
	fǎ xī sī
franc	法朗
	fǎ láng

G

gallon	加仑
	jiā lún
golf	高尔夫球
	gāo ěr fū qiú
Gothic	哥特式建筑
	gē tè shì jiàn zhù
guitar	吉它
	jí tā

H

hamburger	汉堡包
	hàn bǎo bāo
heroin	海洛因
	hǎi luò yīn
hippie	嬉皮士
	xī pí shì

hormone
荷尔蒙
hé ěr méng

hysteria
歇斯底里
xiē sī dǐ lǐ

J

jacket
茄克衫
jiá kè shān

jazz
爵士乐
jué shì yuè

jeep
吉普车
jí pǔ chē

K

karaoke
卡拉ＯＫ
kǎ lā ōu kèi

karst
卡斯特地型
kǎ sī tè dì xíng

KGB
克格勃
kè gé bó

khaki
卡其布
kǎ qí bù

kiss
剋斯
kèi si

L

laser
镭射
léi shè

lemon	柠檬
	níng méng
lemonade	柠檬水
	níng méng shuǐ
logic	逻辑
	luóji

M

mandolin	曼陀林
	màn tuó lín
mango	芒果
	máng guǒ
marathon	马拉松
	mǎ lā sōng
mazurka	玛祖卡
	mǎ zǔ kǎ
Meniere's syndrome	美尼尔氏症
	měi ní ěr shì zhèng
microphone (mike)	麦克风
	mài kè fēng
miniskirt	迷你裙
	mí nǐ qún
model	模特
	mó tè
modern	摩登
	mó dēng
morphine	吗啡
	mǎ fēi
mosaic	马赛克
	mǎ sài kè

motorcycle　　　摩托车
　　　　　　　　mó tuó chē
mousse　　　　　魔丝
　　　　　　　　mó sī

N

Nazi　　　　　　纳粹
　　　　　　　　nà cuì
neon　　　　　　霓虹灯
　　　　　　　　ní hóng dēng
nicotine　　　　尼古丁
　　　　　　　　ní gǔ dīng

O

Olympics　　　　奥林匹克
　　　　　　　　ào lín pí kè
ounce　　　　　　盎司
　　　　　　　　àng sī

P

penicillin　　　盘尼西林
　　　　　　　　pán ní xī lín
pepsi　　　　　　百事（可乐）
　　　　　　　　bǎi shì (kě lè)
peso　　　　　　比索
　　　　　　　　bǐ suǒ
pie (apple pie)　攀（苹果攀）
　　　　　　　　pān (píngguǒ pān)

pizza	比萨饼
	bǐ sà bǐng
Polaroid	拍立得
	pāi lì dé
polka	波尔卡
	bō ěr kǎ
pound	磅
	bàng
pudding	布丁
	bù dīng

Q

quart	夸脱
	kuà tuō

R

radar	雷达
	léi dá
romance	罗曼司
	luó màn sī
romantic	罗曼蒂克
	luó màn dì kè
rupee	卢比
	lú bǐ

S

salad	色拉
	sè lā

salon	沙龙 *shā lóng*
samba	桑巴 *sāng bā*
sandwich	三明治 *sān míng zhì*
sardine	沙丁鱼 *shā dīng yú*
sari	莎丽服 *shā lì fú*
saxophone	萨克管 *sà kè guǎn*
shampoo	香波 *xiāng bō*
soda	苏打 *sū dǎ*
sofa	沙发 *shā fā*
sundae	圣代 *shèng dài*

T

tampax	丹碧丝 *dān bì sī*
tank	坦克 *tǎn kè*
tango	探戈舞 *tān ge wǔ*
TOEFL	托福 *tuō fú*

ton	吨
	dūn
T-shirt	T恤衫
	tì xuě shān

V

Vaseline	凡士林
	fán shì lín
vitamin	维他命
	wéi tā mìng
vodka	伏特加
	fú tè jiā
volt	伏特
	fú tè
Volvo	富豪
	fù háo

W

whiskey	威士忌
	wēi shì jì

X

X-ray	艾克斯光
	ài kè sī guāng

Y

yiddish	依地语
	yī dì yǔ

yoga

瑜伽

yú jiā

yuppie

雅皮士

yǎ pí shì

Appendix II
Computer and Internet Terms

A

alias
别名
bié míng

anonymous FTP
无记名文件存取
wú jì míng wénjiàn cún qǔ

AOL (America Online)
"线上美国"
（电脑服务网）
xiàn shàng Měiguó (diàn nǎo fú wù wǎng)

archie
文件搜寻站
wénjiàn sōu xún zhàn

ascii
美标码
měi biāo mǎ

at sign @
@符
@fú

autoexecutive files
自动执行文件
zì dòng zhí xíng wénjiàn

B

backslash
右斜杠
yòu xié gàng

backup
备份，作备份
bèi fèn, zuò bèi fèn

batch files
批处理文件
pī chù lǐ wén jiàn

binary files　　　二进制文件,二位元文件
èr jìng zhì wén jiàn, èr wèi
yuán wénjiàn

Big 5 codes　　　五大码
wǔ dà mǎ

bitnet　　　比特网
bǐ tè wǎng

browsers　　　浏览器,阅读器
liú lǎn qì, yuè dú qì

C

channel (Internet Relay Chat)
（联网中继聊天）闲谈频道
(lián wǎng zhōng jì liáo tiān)
xián tán pín dào

commands　　　指令，命令
zhǐ lìng, mìng lìng

compressed files　　　压缩文件
yā suō wén jiàn

Compuserve　　　电脑服务网
diàn nǎo fú wù wǎng

computers　　　电脑,计算机
diàn nǎo, jì suàn jī

crashes　　　死机,（机器/程序）瘫痪
sǐ jī, (jī qì/chéng xù) tān huàn

cursor　　　光标
guāng biāo

cyberspace　　　网络空间
wǎng luò kōng jiān

D

database 数据库
shù jù kù

default value 内定值
nèi dìng zhí

default setup 内定设置
nèi dìng shè zhì

Delphi "待尔发"（电脑服务网）
dài ěr fā (diàn nǎo fú wù wǎng)

directory 目录
mù lù

discussion groups 讨论组
tǎo lùn zǔ

domain name 域名，网域地址
yù míng, wǎng yù dì zhǐ

dot character (.) 点符
diǎn fú

download 下载
xià zài

drive 驱动器
qū dòng qì

E

E-mail 电子邮件
diàn zǐ yóu jiàn

error message 出错信息,错误信息
chū cuò xìn xī, cuò wù xìn xī

Ethernet 以太网
yǐ tài wǎng

extensions 扩展名
kuò zhǎn míng

F

FAQ (Frequently Asked Questions)
常见问题
cháng jiàn wèn tí

FTP (file transfer protocol)
文件传输协议,远程存取
wén jiàn chuán shū xié yì,
yuǎn chéng cún qǔ

filename
文件名
wén jiàn míng

files
文件
wén jiàn

finger
人名查询
rén míng chá xún

flame (war)
叫骂（骂战）
jiào mà (mà zhàn)

folder
文件夹
wén jiàn jiā

fonts
字库，字体
zì kù, zì tǐ

format
格式化
gé shì huà

freenet
免费网
miǎn fèi wǎng

G

gopher
考访服务
kǎo fǎng fú wù

gb codes
国标码
guó biāo mǎ

GUI (graphical user interfaces)
图象用户介面
tú xiàng yòng hù jiè miàn
图象使用者介面
tú xiàng shǐ yòng zhě jiè miàn

H

hardware
硬件，硬体
yìng jiàn, yìng tǐ
host
主机
zhǔ jī
http (hypertext transfer protocol)
超文本传送协议
chāo wén běn chuán sòng xié yì
hypertext
超文本
chāo wén běn
hz codes
汉字码
hàn zì mǎ

I

Internet
英特网
yīng tè wǎng
IP address
数字地址
shù zì dì zhǐ
IP (Internet protocol) 联网协议
lián wǎng xié yì
IRC (Internet Relay Chat) 联网中继聊天
lián wǎng zhōng jì liáo tiān

J

Jughead searches　　盲目搜寻
máng mù sōu xún

K

keywords　　检索词
jiǎn suǒ cí

Korn shell　　康氏外壳
kāng shì wài ké

L

LAN (local area networks)　　局域网络,区域网络
jú yù wǎng luò, qū yù wǎng luò

listserv　　邮单服务系统,邮递系统
yóu dān fú wù xì tǒng, yóu dì xì tǒng

login　　载入,连线,上机
zài rù, lián xiàn, shàng jī

logout　　载出,退出连线,注销
zài chū, tuì chū lián xiàn, zhù xiāo

M

mail　　邮件
yóu jiàn

mailing list　　邮单,邮递名单
yóu dān, yóu dì míng dān

main menu	主选单,主菜单
	zhǔ xuǎn dān, zhǔ cài dān
menu	选单,菜单
	xuǎn dān, cài dān
messages	消息
	xiāo xi
modem	调制/解调器,数据机
	tiáo zhì/jiě tiáo qì, shù jù jī
Mosaic	马赛克浏览器
	mǎ sài kè liú lǎn qì
mouse	滑鼠
	huá shǔ
MUD (Multiple User Dimension)	
	多用户
	duō yòng hù
multimedia	多媒体
	duō méi tǐ

N

Netscape	网景浏览器
	wǎng jǐn liú lǎn qì
Network	网络
	wǎng luò
newsgroups	新闻栏
	xīn wén lán
nickname	别名
	bié míng
nodes	结点
	jié diǎn

O

online   线上,网上
                               xiàn shàng, wǎng shàng
Output   输出
                               shū chū

P

paging   呼叫
                               hū jiào
path   路径
                               lù jìn
pipe symbol (|)   转向符（|）
                               zhuǎn xiàng fú (|)
pointer   指向点
                               zhǐ xiàng diǎn
PPP (Point to Point Protocol)
                               点对点（传输）协议
                               *diǎn duì diǎn (chuán shū) xié
                               yì*
Prodigy   "天才"（电脑服务网）
                               *"tiān cái" (diàn nǎo fú wù
                               wǎng)*
programming   程序编写,程式编写
                               *chéng xù biān xiě, chéng shì
                               biān xiě*
protocols   协议,规定程式,规程
                               *xié yì, guī dìng chéng shì, guī
                               chéng*

Q

? (Question mark)　问号
　　　　　　　　wèn hào

R

remote login　远端联机
　　　　　　　yuǎn duān lián jī

Return　回车
　　　　　huí chē

RFC (Request for comment)
　　　　征求意见（书/信）
　　　　zhēng qiú yì jiàn (shū/xìn)

Root directories　根目录
　　　　　　　　gēn mù lù

routers　路由器
　　　　　lù yóu qì

S

Scroll　卷动
　　　　juǎn dòng

Search　搜寻
　　　　　sōu xún

server/client　服务器/客户
　　　　　　　fú wù qì/kè hù

SLIP (Serial Line Internet Protocol)
　　　　互联网串行线（传输）协议
　　　　hù lián wǎng chuàn xíng
　　　　xiàn (chuán shū) xié yì

shell	外壳（程序）
	wài ké (chéng xù)
slash (/)	左斜杠
	zuǒ xié gàng
smileys ：·)	笑脸符号
	xiào liǎn fú hào
subdirectory	子目录
	zǐ mù lù

T

talk program	对谈程序
	duì tán chéng xù
TCP/IP (Transmission Control Protocol/Internet Protocol)	传输控制/网内协议
	chuán shū kòng zhì/wǎng nèi xié yì
telnet	远程载入,远程登录
	yuǎn chéng zài rù, yuǎn chéng dēng lù
threads	相关文章
	xiāng guān wén zhāng

U

uncompress	解压缩
	jiě yā suō
Unix	Unix 操作系统
	Unix *cāo zuò xì tǒng*
upload	上载
	shàng zài

usenet	用户网
	yòng hù wǎng
userids	用户账号
	yòng hù zhàng hào
utility programs	实用程序
	shí yòng chéng xù
Unicode	统一码
	tǒng yī mǎ

V

variables	变数，变量
	biàn shù, biàn liàng
vector fonts	向量字库，矢量字库
	xiàng liàng zì kù, shǐ liàng zì kù
Veronica searches	维洛尼卡检索
	wéi luò ní kǎ jiǎn suǒ
virtual reality	虚拟实景
	xū nǐ shí jǐn

W

Wais (Wide Area Information Service)
广域资讯服务
guǎng yù zī xùn fú wù

Wan (Wide Area Networks)
广域网
guǎng yù wǎng

word processor	词处理软件
	cí chù lǐ ruǎn jiàn

WWW (World Wide Web)
万维网
wàn wéi wǎng

Whois
地址查询
dì zhǐ chá xún

X

X window
X 视窗
X *shì chuāng*

Z

zip files
压缩文件
yā suō wén jiàn

zmodem
zmodem 传输方式
zmodem *chuán shū fāng shì*

Chinese Phonetic Guide

1. Pronunciation Guide for Chinese in both *Pinyin* and Wade-Giles

(All English phonemes according to standard US English)

Pinyin	Wade-Giles	Equivalent English Phoneme
a	a	"o" as in "dot"
b	p	"b" as in "big"
c	ts	"ts" as in "hats"
d	t	"d" as in "radar"
e	er	no English phoneme; "oe" as in French "oevre"
f	f	"f" as in "feather"
g	k	"g" as in "god"
h	h	"h" as in "hot"
i (before n)	i or ih	"i" as in "pin"
i (after sh)	ih	"ur" as in "purr"
i (after other consonants)	i or ee	"ee" as in "sweet"
j	ch	"j" as in "jar"
k	k'	"k" as in "kite"
l	l	"l" as in "limp"
m	m	"m" as in "moan"
n	n	"n" as in "nut"
o	aw	"o" as in "frog"

p	p'	"p" as in "pig"
q	ch'	"ch" as in "chest"
r	j	"j" as in "jug"

(Chinese has a second "r"-like sound as well with no equivalent English phoneme)

s	s	"s" as in "sex"
t	t'	"t" as in "toy"
u	eu	"oo" as in "moon"
w	w	"w" as in "wand"
x	hs	"sh" as in "she"
y	io	"y" as in "young"
z	tz	"dz" as in "words"
ai	i	"y" as in "buy"
ao	au	"ou" as in "proud"
ei	ay or ai	"ay" as in "lay"
ia	ya or ia	"ya" as in "yard"
iao	yao or iao	"eow" as in "meow"
iu	iu	"yo" as in "yo-yo"
ui	uay or uai	"way" as in "sway"
uo	aw	"aw" as in "saw"
ng	ng	"ng" as in "hang"
sh	shr	"shr" as in "shrimp"
zh	dz, tz, or dh	no equivalent phoneme; halfway between "dr" as in "drop" and "dz" as in "words"

2. Tones

The Chinese language has different tones that are capable of differentiating meanings. Differences in tone convey different meanings to otherwise identical or similar syllables. In the Beijing dialect, which Mandarin Chinese is based on, there are four basic tones, which are written as follows, using the syllable *"ba"* as an example:

First tone: represented by the tone-graph " ⁻ ", a high, level pitch. *Bā* (八) in this tone can mean the number 8.

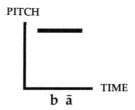

Second tone: represented by the tone-graph " ´ ", it is a rising tone, starting about mid-range of a speaker's voice, and ending slightly above the first tone. *Bá* (拔) can mean "to uproot".

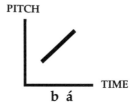

Third tone: represented by the tone-graph " ˇ ", it is a dipping pitch, falling from mid-range to low, then rising. *Bǎ* (把) can mean "to hold".

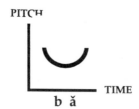

Fourth tone: represented by the tone-graph " ˋ ", it is a sharply falling pitch, starting near the top of the speaker's range and reaching mid- to low-level at the end. *Bà* (霸) can mean "tyrant" or "despot".

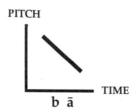

Besides, brief, unstressed syllables may also occur and take a feeble tone, such as *ba* (吧). They have no tone mark.